QAnon: The Battle for Earth And Our Souls
The Awakening Begins

QVeritas

Legal Disclaimer

This book is copyright © 2018 by QVeritas with all rights reserved. It is illegal to copy, distribute, or create derivative works from this book in whole or in part or to contribute to the copying, distribution, or creating of derivative works of this book.

No part of this report may be reproduced or transmitted in any form whatsoever, electronic, or mechanical, including photocopying, recording, or by any informational storage or retrieval system without expressed written, dated and signed permission from the author.

DEDICATION

This book is dedicated to all those who are looking for truth, those who are wondering why the condition of this world is so unbalanced, who want to look behind the illusions and lies, those who see injustice in the world and demand justice.

This book was written as a contribution to the fight of the righteous and the never-ending hope for a better future.

You are not alone, there is still good in the world, even if sometimes it does not seem so.

As you go through each day, remember that answers always lie ahead and some of them will be in this book.

        The truth is out there and inside you.

TABLE OF CONTENTS

Introduction

Chapter 1 – A Divided Society United by Q
A World In Seeming Disarray
More People are Starting to Wake Up
The Deep State And Why Trump is Working Hard to End Them
The Stirrings of the QAnon Movement
It All Began with Q
The Birth of QAnon
QAnon And His Relationship With Trump

Chapter 2 – The Most Popular of Q's Breadcrumbs
The Storm – The Secret Plan to Decimate the Top Members of the Deep State
The Story of the Mockingbird
Deep State's Puppet Masters – Soros, Rothschild, and House of Saud
Is Kim Jong-un of North Korea a CIA puppet?
The Plot to Murder Seth Rich
The Real Objective of the Mueller Investigation
The Sinking of the Titanic – How J.P. Morgan got rid of his rivals
The Child Sex Ring Issue
Red October
The Cover-Up of the Death of Justice Ruth Bader
The Execution of John McCain

Chapter 3- Looking into Q
Theories About Q's Identity
Q might be a hoax but the hype is Real
Q was not alone
The Other People that Fanned the QAnon flames
Why People Believe Q
How The Q Phenomenon Has Affected The Real World

Chapter 4 – The Fall of Q?
The Failed Predictions or So Some Think
QAnon-related Incidents that put the Movement in Bad Light
Mainstream Media's Takes a closer Look at QAnon's origin
Access denied for Q and his followers
Anonymous promises to get Q
Conclusion
Sources

INTRODUCTION

Almost all the evil on Earth is caused by a cabal of international elites. This group is composed of top personalities in Hollywood, politicians from the Democratic Party, and certain factions of the intelligence agencies. This group is known as the Deep State. It is said to be the entity behind the 9/11 attack, JFK assassination, the Susurluk scandal, and countless other violent episodes in history. Or so some people believe.

With a global entity as strong as this one, what chance does the world have of overcoming this evil? What if I told you that something is already being done? A group has begun moving in order to combat Deep State. Their weapon? Donald Trump. It is said that Trump was selected from a pool of possible heroes by a small group of powerful entities, allegedly connected to the military, that are sick and tired of the machinations of Deep State. They chose Trump because he is rich enough that he is able to block the influence of Deep State. He cannot be paid or swayed.

The battle between the two groups nearly came to a head when Deep State attempted to shoot down the

President's airplane in order to foil Trump's meeting with North Korean leader, Kim Jong-Un.

Why do they want to get rid of Trump so badly? This is because Trump is readying a killing blow to his opponents, starting from unleashing thousands of indictments which will send top-tier Deep State personalities such as Barack Obama and Hillary Clinton to jail. Luckily, the attempt to down Air Force One failed.

Is this all true? According to QAnon and its (his?) believers, all these are factual. Who is QAnon and why does this anonymous entity know so much about the machinations of Trump versus the Deep State? Many are wondering if the information that Q has been dropping is legitimate. Many more are dead sure that Q is dropping these crumbs so believers can aid their hero in finally defeating Deep State.

The public is divided. Some dismiss the notion that there is such a person who is close enough to Trump that he knows what the president is going to say in his next speech. They view this movement as a hoax designed for some unknown purpose. Maybe it is designed so a certain few can make a tidy profit by fooling the gullible.

While another faction believes that there is indeed an insider, possibly more than one, who is working closely with the nation's highest leader. The insider is privy to the most secret plans that the president is hatching. They think that Q knows that the president cannot do this alone, the act of dismantling Deep State and making America great again. That is why he is reaching out to possible allies.

Mainstream media considers it the craziest conspiracy

theory to ever hit the US. The story behind the movement has all the elements of a great spy movie. There's a secret society made up of the world's most powerful and richest people. They are evil. And evil here doesn't mean they avoid paying their taxes. Think pedophilia, child trafficking, and murder. This group is willing to do anything and everything not only to stay in power, but also to keep everyone under theirs.

Then there is this leader, Donald Trump, who has been chosen to take down this group. He has been hand picked by the military to lead their offense against the cabal – the Deep State. This leader appears clueless, even incompetent at times. But it is all an act. He appears like he doesn't know what he is doing so Deep State would underestimate him. He needs them to underestimate him in order for him to do his job – to bring down the top people of the cabal.

There are also the people. The people have long been programmed to believe whatever others in power tell them. These people are unaware that there is a group that controls their lives. The cabal has a say on what they eat, what medicine they take, what work they take on, which news they watch, everything. They have been conditioned to just accept that they are poor because of their choices, that they are sick because of their actions, and that they are powerless to change the world. Until one day, a certain entity reached out and helped the people open their eyes.

This is the final character in this movie-like scenario – the anonymous insider that serves as a liaison to the outside world. This insider is simply known as QAnon. Q knows everything that is happening inside Trump's camp. He knows that all this blustering and bumbling in the White

House is done for show. He wants the people to know this, to give them hope, and to validate their decision for voting for him. Q also wants to warn people that there will be upheavals in the coming days. It will be messy, and many will be taken down as collateral damage. QAnon wants the people, those who are now awake, to be aware of what is happening so that they can keep themselves and their families safe.

This seems like one thrilling movie, right? The problem is, this is not a movie. It is real life. We are all part of it. And if we don't wake up, we might be taken down with Deep State in the cleansing that Q claims is about to take place.

There are some real-world consequences to the things that are happening between these factions. This book will let you see both sides of the battling groups. If you have heard of the QAnon movement and want to learn more about this growing movement, this book is for you.
If you are one of the sceptics and you want to learn why people would believe such crazy notions, this book is also for you. It exposes the good and the bad about the movement. This book will not try to convince you to believe that what Q is saying is true. It only wants to present all the facts so that you can make your own conclusions. That's what Q is all about, anyway. He presents all the facts. It is up to you to interpret it. You have to connect the dots to see how each player fits into the narrative. He doesn't expect you to believe everything. He only wants people to start being more aware of the truth.

This book, QAnon: The Battle for Earth And Our

Souls - The Awakening Begins, will give you an introduction to the QAnon Phenomenon. We will take a look at:

• What Deep State is in the context of the United States
• Who are the key players in this ongoing battle between the government and the secret cabal of evil entities?
• Who is QAnon?
• Where did this all start?
• What are the clues the Q Anon left us and what they could possibly mean?
• How did the QAnon movement affect the world?

If you, like thousands of other people who want to understand what is truly happening in the world, want to delve deeper into the history and workings of the movement and desire to explore the possibilities that we may have been fooled by an all-powerful entity into believing the truths they manufactured, then you have to download this book as soon as possible.

This book will also take a closer look at the apparent fall of the QAnon movement. Mainstream media claims that the phenomenon, while meteoric in its rise, is also quick to burn out. There are countless articles published claiming that Q is just a hoax, a game gone awry, a publicity stunt for alt-right personalities, and so much more. Some chapters will look into uncovering of the possible identities of Q. It also has chapters on:

• What the mainstream media has dug up about QAnon
• The failed predictions of Q
• The supposed suppression of the QAnon movement
• Acts of violence associated with QAnon followers

These are perceived to have contributed to what appears like the downfall of Q. Is this the end of Q, or is the end just the beginning?

CHAPTER 1 – A DIVIDED SOCIETY UNITED BY Q

A World In Seeming Disarray

In a 2018 edition of a US publication, New Yorker, a telling article appeared. The story claims that a large population of people all over the world now believe that our planet is flat. Yes. There is now a huge number of individuals who believe that what we have been taught in our science classes for decades is false. Never mind the numerous studies that have disproved this ancient belief. Never mind the pictures from satellites showing that the Earth is indeed a sphere.

Central to this flat-earth belief is the idea that the moon landing is fake. In fact, many believe that space flight, together with other long-proven scientific principles, has been faked by a certain group. To what end? This remains unclear. But Flat Earthers are sure that we have been fed with false information for many, many years now.

During a flat-earther conference, a speaker claimed that "facts" can no longer be trusted because the source of these facts may have motivations that are unknown to its receivers. Majority of the information that we have been receiving from what was previously believed to be reputable bodies can no longer be accepted at face value.

The speaker goes on to ask his audience if they have been to Jupiter? If they have seen Jupiter with their own eyes? He then asks them why they are too quick to accept that Jupiter exists when their own senses have not proven its existence. He goes on to say that the audience should go back to trusting their senses rather than believing any person who claims to know the truth. [1]

This may sound like a bad episode of the television series, The X-Files. It is not. Today's environment of post-truths and alternative facts have made the ground fertile for an increasing collection of alternate theories.

Another prevalent "fact" that is now also being challenged is the efficacy and safety of vaccines. News outlets have been reporting that in the US alone, there is an outbreak, some the largest their state has seen in over thirty years, of measles. The reason? Because parents are now choosing to not have their children immunized due to the fact that vaccines are more harmful than good.

Despite a large body of evidence favoring vaccination in preventing illnesses, people are still choosing to skip it. Despite doctors campaigning about the effectivity of vaccines in preventing unnecessary outbreaks, the number of children that are going unvaccinated is growing. Despite states mandating students to get their injections, parents simply aren't budging on this topic.

The same is true for climate change. Certain individuals who are commonly labeled as climate change deniers firmly believe that the earth is not becoming warmer. They are sure that scientists are tweaking their data just to scare people. To what end? To influence policy makers to take certain steps that most are not aware of.

These unpopular belief systems have been labeled as "conspiracy theories" and those who believe in them are seen to be gullible and uneducated. But lately, even scientists and other academics have begun to come out and support these beliefs. Doctors claiming that they do not have their children vaccinated have become more vocal particularly on social media. Scientists have come forward with their own studies to prove that the Earth is still the same temperature as it was decades ago.

Wide-open media brought about by the digital age has a huge hand in this "phenomenon". With information, whether true or false, made so easily accessible, people are having a more difficult time assessing whether what they are reading is factual or not. This incubates the notion of paranoia.

The public begins to wonder whether they are being made to think the way they do by a powerful entity. They wonder whether the information that they are reading are so designed or presented to that they would act or think the way a certain group wants them to. Nobody is quick to believe anything. People have begun to question each piece of information that they are handed.

The problem is, what if the paranoia is warranted? Who is to say that people are not being manipulated by the media? With the imbalance of power and wealth so great, there are individuals who can afford to pay for news outlets to publish their "truths". Who will help us correct this imbalance? For the longest time, people have been looking for an entity who can and will tell us the truth.

There are now numerous pundits who explore the various possibilities that a "truth" is not the actual truth. They spend countless hours finding out which entity or group benefits if the masses accept the truth that has been put forth. No one has been established yet as the ultimate gatekeeper of truths, not until one shadowy entity emerged from the murky pool of a fairly unknown imageboard. This entity is Q.

MORE PEOPLE ARE STARTING TO WAKE UP

Nowadays, people are exposed to many shades of truth. People are also told so many lies. Some lies are so outrageous that many automatically reject them. Other lies are so close to truths that they enter a grey area where people cannot readily reject nor accept them. Many alternate theories fall under that grey area.

The reason why people find so many things, even outrageous information, difficult to dismiss is that there have been many instances when the outrageous turned out to be true. When the difference between what is true and what is not gets blurred so very well, it becomes impossible to just accept information to be true or dismiss what is absurd as a lie.

One example of a theory that seemed so absurd was the MK-Ultra Project. In 1953, the US Central Intelligence Agency started working on a clandestine project called MK-Ultra. It aimed to develop a truth serum and other interrogation processes to be used on humans. They were created for the purpose of weakening suspected spies and forcing them to confess secrets by way of mind control.

This project involved illegal activities like administration of LSD, sensory deprivation, isolation, hypnosis, sexual abuse, and other kinds of torture on unwitting test subjects from the US and Canada. It was reportedly halted twenty years after its inception but there are still some people who believe that the program simply went underground. [2]

Project MK-Ultra is one example of activities that seem so horrific that it would seem impossible to be true. But it is and is now public knowledge thanks largely to a report on the New York Times back in 2974. If you lived during that time and somebody told you that he was being forced by the government to take drugs in order to control his mind, you probably would immediately tell that person to get help from a psychiatrist. Nowadays, people will not be too quick to dismiss this. Yes, while many would still look at you like a crazy person, a number of people around you will seek for more proof. There are more people who are open to the possibility that the absurd may also have a grain of truth.

Another conspiracy theory that was prevalent back in the day was that former Beatle member, John Lennon, was being spied on by the FBI. His fans could not believe that a person as popular yet as unthreatening as Lennon could ever attract the attention of this bureau. As it turns out, he was just one of over a dozen notable celebrities that were being constantly watched by the group. He was placed on the "possible threat" list because he wrote the song "Give Peace a Chance".

Apparently, then president Richard Nixon did not appreciate the anti-war sentiments of the song. Additionally, Lennon met with some anti-war activists during his visit to New York in 1971. It was at this time that the FBI placed Lennon on their watch list. INS even tried to have the singer deported one year later. Theories swirled around about the surveillance that the intelligence group placed on the Beatle member. It was Jon Weiner, a historian, who spent a total of fourteen years trying to gain access to the secret files the FBI had on Lennon. Weiner had to take this to the Supreme Court before the FBI agreed to release their files. [3]

Need another proof that sometimes, conspiracy theories that sound incredible actually are true? What about the time when people began saying that there are entities spying on you through your computer's own camera? Anybody who has access to the Internet must have come across this notion at least once in his or her life. While some dismiss it as an idea that only the paranoid entertains, there is actually truth in it.

In 2014, a huge cyber operation was conducted by the FBI. This operation resulted in the apprehension of scores of webcam hackers from more than a dozen countries worldwide. The hackers used the program Blackshades in order to gain access to their victims' computers and all the files and photographs in its memory. The program also enables the hackers to record keystrokes of the users. This enabled them to steal the passwords to their victims' accounts.

The most horrifying capability of Blackshades is that it allowed the hackers to activate the web camera on the victim's computer without alerting the owner of the machine. Ironically, the FBI is also accused of hacking into certain individual's computers in order to gain access to their computers' webcams. They have been known to do this as part of their surveillance practices. [4]

So, if you notice a friend or a relative covering their laptop's web camera with tape, do you dismiss their paranoia and laugh at them? Do you call them crazy for believing the theories that somebody could be watching them through their computers?

This is the type of ridicule that QAnon and its believers are experiencing right now. Add to the fact that whenever a conspiracy theory arises, it is portrayed mostly as negative by mainstream media. Their presentation of an unconventional information is largely, "this is crazy and whoever believes this must be crazy too." The pejorative tone discourages people from exploring any truth behind the theory for fear of being perceived as somebody insane.

The good thing with the Internet is that mainstream media no longer has sole control over which information gets served to the public. Anybody who has a truth to reveal can go online and talk about it. Whether it is on a personal blog or a social media account, a person or organization can reveal the things that they know. This free access to information and the ability to get your message out so easily is the reason why more and more people are waking up.

It is difficult to control the narrative, the truth when the public has access to information that contradicts what you are trying to feed them. Access gives people the power to analyze information from all sides and decide on their own truth.

And for a growing number of people, the truth is that Deep State is doing everything in its power to keep the truth of their existence and machinations under wraps. The truth is the government, led by Donald Trump, is doing everything in its power to thwart these rogue individuals. And there is one entity, QAnon, who is hell-bent on revealing these truths to anyone who is willing to look.

THE DEEP STATE AND WHY TRUMP IS WORKING HARD TO END THEM

The term "Deep State" has been around for many years but only took off as part of the American lexicon in 2016. The term was bandied about in small circles to refer to a group that is opposing the mainstream candidates. In 2017, after his inauguration, President Trump and his close associates started using the term more frequently to describe people or groups that are opposing him.

The concept of Deep State was originally used to refer to a shadow government that operated in Turkey, Pakistan, and Egypt. The authoritarian elements in these countries worked together in order to undercut those leaders who were democratically elected. The groups engaged in violent acts and disseminated propaganda in order to undermine the ruling government party. The group often coordinated with people who were outside of the government.

In the US, a particular study polling the public yielded that 37% of the total number of people interviewed have heard of the term "Deep State". When they were asked if they think there was a group, other than the elected government, that secretly manipulated national policies, more than half of the participants said that they believe there is indeed a secret group that was pulling the strings.

Studies suggest that American Deep State originated in 1947 as a result of the creation of the NSA or National Security Act. This was signed by then president Truman as part of the government's improvement during the Cold War. The establishment of this department was done in secret and was kept a secret for over a decade. The newly formed body became crucial in initiating security policies as well as advising the president, and future presidents. Its influence was huge and only grew bigger over the years.

It was said that the American government had always maintained secrets, amassed bits of intelligence, and engaged in wars. With the creation of the NSA, these secrets became more important as they were used in prosecuting people that endangered the security of the country. Theorists claimed that the Deep State in the US was not intentionally malevolent. It has changed to be what it is today due to structural incentives. While it operated covertly before, Deep State has changed into an entity that operated overtly, in plain sight.

While secrecy is still important, the citizens seem to have accepted that corporation men have joined the lobby. Interest groups and lobbyists create bills and they put into power politicians that vote on them. Public concerns such as universal health care and climate change do not get noticed because bodies with powerful interests want it that way. Now, the policies that get pushed forward are the ones that keep the influential and powerful in their position.

Experts in political science tell us that governance, not just in the US but all over the world, has been divided into two groups, a professor named Michael Glennon named the two Madisonian and Trumanite. The Madisonian were politicians, like the president and the senators, that are charged with making sure that democratic governance exists, and they act based on the will of the citizenry.

Trumanite on the other hand, are officials who are deeply in bed with national security and owe their power and authority to the NSA. They are said to have power over the security state. They work to ensure the continuity of policies from the former administration to the next. These two bodies think that are each working for the betterment of the State, but their mandate varies. This is the reason why the two groups butt head most of the time. [5]

Freedom House, an advocacy group for human, political, and democratic rights, maintains that the Deep State has a seriously sinister meaning. They have mafia leaders controlling certain military leaders to kill and torture members of the minority. In the American setting, Deep State is seen as a collection of individuals that are part of both the private and public sectors that manipulate government policies. Again, they have a hand I running the lives of the masses so that everybody else stays poor, ignorant, and sick. This way, the people will be too busy dealing with their lives to care about anything bigger. This is how Deep State stays in power.

Since Trump has been elected, Q claims that he has been taking steps in order to take apart this organization. For the longest time, Deep State has gone unopposed. With the entrance of Trump, there is now a huge stumbling block for the cabal. Q claims that whatever Trump is doing is proving to be a huge threat to the existence of Deep State. Several individuals believe that the Deep State is targeting Trump. In fact, a journalist claimed that in January of 2018 Deep State "unleashed" what can be considered as its most aggressive and tawdriest attempt to assault Donald Trump when news that Russia has compromising information regarding the nation's president.

According to intelligence officials, certain Russian personalities meddled in the 2016 presidential election in order to aid Trump in his candidacy. Trump quickly dismissed this conclusion and has directed his staff to investigate this Moscow influence to find out if Obama has organized an effort to infiltrate his office and spy on him. Who is Deep State exactly? While Donald Trump himself has never uttered the term in a public setting, he has been known to allude to it. On his Twitter account in 2018, Trump accused former president Barack Obama of having the Trump Tower wiretapped before the 2016 elections. This claim of Trump is actually a federal crime.

There are many safeguards in place that prevents even the head of state to order this form of surveillance. However, there must be a reason why this theory keeps on resurfacing over and over again. Is there a grain of truth to this claim? If yes, when will it be revealed to the public? This claim against Obama is not the only instance that people in the government has connected the former president to the Deep State. People around Trump believe that members of the Deep State are holdovers from the former administration. These are longtime workers in the government that are loyal to the former people in power and are actively working to threaten the presidency and undermine Trump.

Sean Spicer, White House's Press Secretary, was quick to explain that he finds it unsurprising should there be an existing Deep State. He said that if you have worked for one party in office for eight years and you believe in the agenda of that administration, you will stay affiliated with that group and press to espouse that particular agenda.

When he was asked as to what the government, particularly the CIA, will be doing in order to purge the members and key actors of Deep State, Press Secretary Spicer claimed that doing such a thing is not part of the CIA's mandate.

While Spicer was being a little more careful in alluding to the fact that he believes Obama is part of Deep State, Rep. Mike Kelly is not as shy about his claim. He claimed that the former president and his family chose to live in Washington in order to continue to undermine Donald Trump's presidency. The Pennsylvania representative stated in an interview that Obama is in the state solely to organize the "shadow government" and derail the new agenda.

It is known by many that the family of Barack Obama elected to lease a home in Washington after going out of office so that the youngest daughter of the family could finish high school there. When asked for proof, Kelly simply remarked that federal employees left over from the Obama-era has been rejecting Trump's administration's directives. This is seen as orchestrated by the person that they are most loyal to.

Another representative, this time from Iowa, is also tagging Barrack Obama as a major player in the Deep State. Just like Kelly, Rep. Steve King has gone on record accusing the former president of attempting to frustrate Mr. Trump's agenda. He goes on to say that the current president should take steps in order to purge all the leftists inside his administration.

According to Mr. Peter Feaver, a civil-military issues expert, there is a long history of American governments butting heads with the federal bureaucracy. President Richard Nixon also had a form of distrust of the government and felt that it was out to get him at times. He adds that it is not new news for warring factions within the government to exhibit dissent.

As an example, he noted that George P. Shultz, then secretary of state, and Caspar Weinberger, the secretary of defense during Ronal Regan's administration, often found themselves at odds with each other and would duel on the news.

An adviser of Trump's administration, James Carafano, tried to find a middle ground. He claims that just because sensitive information is leaking and there are obstructions in Trump's policies, it doesn't automatically mean that a Deep State exists.

Time and time again, evidence of such leakage and opposition have existed and it is not unique to this administration. Because there is no solid evidence to prove its existence, it becomes difficult to tell. Is the Deep State theory simply being used by the current administration as a scapegoat for its inabilities or is it an actual, valid theory?

A professor from Duke University who has studied what

has occurred in Turkey, Timur Kuran, has said that leaks of information would only prove a presence of Deep State if there was conclusive proof that they are all connected not just to each other but also to a conspiratorial scheme. So far, there are no shreds of evidence of that. Leaks of information are proof that there are some people who are dissatisfied with the bureaucracy and are upset over certain policies.

The existence of this individual is not enough proof of an organizational hierarchy that is moving to systematically destabilize the government. According to David Gergen, a presidential adviser for several terms now, President Trump came with a mandate to rip up the US government's old model – the very same model that these civil servants have worked hard to build over what could be their entire careers. Naturally, there will be some form of pushback. That's what happens when you change the status quo. But is this the work of a Deep State?

In other literature, Deep State takes on a more horrifying meaning. They use the term cabal to describe the group. And they are viewed to control everything. They are out to get rid of the majority of the world's population. And the rest? They want to enslave. They do this through debt-enslavement. If the cabal keeps the majority of the population poor, the people are not going to be able to look at the bigger picture.

They will be too busy working for a living and basically fighting for survival. They are fed food that are laced with chemicals. They take medicine that are designed to make them weak. The school system teaches them just enough to be able to work but ignorant enough to not start asking important questions. The cabal works to keep the status quo going. People work, they save, they become prosperous. And then everything is taken away through war or the imposition of higher taxes. That is why the group has been hard at work to start another great war.

If this happens, the poor will remain poor and those in power will have more time to stay in it. This is what the great awakening is said to be all about. It is trying to open the eyes of more and more people so that we, united, can fight what is established as the New World Order.
This could be the real reason why we need to stop the Deep State. These entities are said to be working to take away what we all see as freedom. Thanks to easier access to information, all types of them, there are more movements now to be aware of what is truly happening around us. Thankfully, there are entities that came into power that want to stop Deep State as well. With their guiding hand, they allegedly chose a hero that has the money and influence to potentially damage and hopefully finally bring down Deep State.

THE STIRRINGS OF THE QANON MOVEMENT

During rallies, it is common to see people holding up signs for others to read. As people watched the news coverage on one of President Trump's rally to campaign for Republican Representative Ron DeSantis in Florida, they noticed something peculiar. Instead of the familiar "Trump 2020" and "Women for Trump" signs, a new one has cropped up.

In the crowd, signs saying "We are Q" were held up by various individuals. Some journalists also noted that a number of people in the audience were wearing t-shirts with the word "QAnon" in the front. Yet another held a cryptic message stating "Q WWG1WGA" with a kicker of "Keep America Great!". These were followed by signs stating that mainstream media is the enemy. What was this group about? Some people thought that it was an organization that is working to promote Trump. While this may be true, the group of Q is more than that.

These placards and shirts refer to a growing movement that is increasingly becoming popular particularly among those that belong to the far-right group. The entire movement, if it can be called that, has been called a "conspiracy cult" and "a grassroots movement" that is slowly exposing the hidden battles between President Trump and the Deep State.

QAnon is a shifting and growing theory that began as an ultra-fringe concept posted in the online message boards. These sites were frequented by alt-right members. Now that it has gotten bigger and its reach has widened, their messages are now available on mainstream platforms such as Reddit, YouTube, Facebook, and Twitter.

The movement's beliefs are anchored on the assertion that Trump is an all-seeing, omnipotent entity. Their main theory is that President Trump has been selected in order to bring back goodness into this world. That he is only acting like a buffoon and seemed to be making so many mistakes to prevent his enemies from realizing what a genius he really is.

For example, when the Mueller inquiry was instigated, it was said to be an investigation to establish if the Trump campaign indeed colluded with the Russian government. According to QAnon beliefs, this is just a charade of sorts.

Q followers believe that Trump controlled the Mueller investigation in order to target certain individuals belonging to the Democratic party, as well as a few Hollywood names, for their involvement with the Deep state, sex rings, and other controversial and illegal activities. It also implicates huge pharmaceutical companies for taking part in activities that are meant to keep the American people drugged and unaware.

Members of QAnon believe that there is a certain individual, Q, who is slowly but surely revealing the extent of the plot. Each revelation is said to be confirmed by parsing selected parts of the president's public speeches. The term that Q believers use for this movement is "the Great Awakening".

While some view this awakening as the revealing of the true nature of people who used to be honored for what was perceived as their contributions to the world, others say that the awakening is the "opening of the eyes" of the masses. The awakening is the unveiling of all the lies that used to be taken as gospel truth.

Leading this awakening is President Trump. He is using the US military and the National Security Agency in order to wage a secret war against the powerful globalists. Another part of the awakening is the restoration of Reaganite family values in America.

QAnon members see this war literally as the ultimate battle between evil and good. And the Awakening is just the beginning. They believe that ones the evil has been dispersed and all that are responsible are already in jail, Trump will take the next step to make the country even greater than it is now.

IT ALL BEGAN WITH Q

Early in October of 2017, Trump had a meeting with senior military officials together with their spouses at the White House. During their dinner, Trump and the officials talked about key national security issues that the country was facing. He talked about the situation in Iran. After dinner, the group had to do the usual picture-taking.

As the group was posing for pictures, Trump casually mentioned that what is happening could be the calm before a "storm". He then exclaims that the greatest military minds were all in the room. When the reporters started inquiring as to what storm he was talking about, they received a cryptic "You'll find out" answer from the nation's leader. Videos of that particular instance circulated online, prompting some major concern from citizens.

A lot of people believed that he was alluding to going to war against Iran. The president did not expound on his declarations that day and the days after. No word about that storm has emerged yet, but people started talking about it.

Some were not overly worried about Trump's statement. He is known for making outrageous and scandalous remarks that nobody seems to see the point of. He is also known to make remarks that would make him appear relevant. At that time, reporters believed that he was trying to show off to the members of the military that was around him. Others believed that there was more to his remark. There were debates online that discussed his statement to no end.

Among those who started talking about the calm before the unknown storm, no one stirred the pot more than Q. [6]

A little under three weeks after that incident, an anonymous individual identified as "Q Clearance Patriot" started posting messages on a /pol/ in 4Chan. This website has seen more than its share of outrageous claims. It is known as an anonymous, post-anything, shadowy website. A newspaper group once called the people in 4Chan juvenile, lunatic, ridiculous, brilliant, and alarming.

The website is the home of political extremism and cruel hoaxes due to the type of posts that are seen on its boards. The name of the imageboard itself, /pol/ is short for "politically incorrect". While the people who are on this channel are not unaccustomed to reading wild accusations against the government and other outrageous claims on the message board, Q's posts slowly but surely garnered attention and kept it.

What is his thread title? It was "Calm before the Storm". The name, Q, was widely believed to refer to Q access authorization or the Q clearance from the US Department of Energy. Simply put, this level of clearance grants the holder access to Restricted Data including utilization, design, and manufacture of atomic weapons.

The Anon in the term "QAnon" refers to the individual Q, who remains anonymous to this day, and the countless nameless supporters of this individual. While a lot of alternate theories rise and fall in the world of 4Chan, QAnon managed to stay alive for nearly two years. Why is this? IS it because Q knew how to give his audience just enough to keep their interests? Or is because people are awake enough to see that the person at the other end knows his stuff, unlike other theorists?

Followers wait for Q's entries to be posted. They believe that Q is using the website to secretly keep the public abreast of President Trump's masterplan in eliminating the members and the leaders of the Deep State. When people started questioning whether Q really existed and whether he was really an insider, he showed the readers proof that he was with the President on Air Force One by posting a blurry picture of a few islands. This coincided with Trump's trip to Asia. [7]

What does Q post? He reveals top-secret details in clue form. Eventually, these clues were labeled as "breadcrumbs". It was the readers on 4Chan who became the "bakers" of Q – the ones who put together the "breadcrumbs" that was posted and turned it into a "dough". The breadcrumbs are very hard to interpret as they appear to be a cross between ransom note and poetry. As an example, look at what Q posted in June of 2018.

After the bakers studied the dropped crumbs, they put their own spin to it and post it on their individual accounts. They talk about it on Reddit. They post videos of their interpretation on YouTube. They share links of other bakers' analysis on Facebook. This is how the QAnon movement grew.

There has been some discussion as to the possibility of Q being just a handle that is managed by a group of people that are indeed close to the president. According to some analysts, Q's posts often refer to the author in the third person pronoun "we". Additionally, the posts go through several changes in style, sentence structure, and syntax. There is still no proof today whether there is some truth to this multiple-Q theory. [8]

THE BIRTH OF QANON

The QAnon movement did not start out with a bang. In fact, you can say that it only started with whispers. These whispers were done online on an imageboard that was frequented by what society considers as outcasts. These people were the perfect audience for Q because they are not your typical reader. These people are used to hoaxes so they are not easily swayed by what can be considered as crazy ramblings from someone pretending to have access to information that even the vice president of the United States may not have. After spending some time in the fringes, the QAnon movement began to seep into the mainstream.

Q silently emerged from the recesses of 4chan. This is an imageboard website where users can post anonymously. 4chan is divided into different boards that have their own content type and guidelines. It is important to note that this English-language site has been linked to internet activism and is the birthplace of many subcultures such as alt-right, Anonymous, and Project Chanology. The users of 4chan are the ones responsible for the creation and popularization of memes like Pedobear, lolcats, and Rickrolling. These people have been described by The Guardian as "juvenile… brilliant… alarming". [9]

Q's very first entry was posted under the "Mueller Investigation" thread. This was found on the board known as /pol/. This first entry was logged on October 28, 2017. Q proceeded to post on various threads before the emergence of a new thread – Breadcrumbs - Q Clearance Patriot.

Q has long since grown to be a huge phenomenon, not just in the US but all over the world. Millions of people wait for his breadcrumbs and hundreds diligently do their research in order to analyze and interpret what Q means. As of 2019, there are over a thousand articles written about QAnon and the movement. Most that are written about Q and his followers are hostile towards Q and the people who believe in his drops.

Some are dismissive and see the QAnon movement as conspiracy theorists who will grab at straws. Still, others believe in what Q has to say and devote themselves to spreading his words. They tweet and retweet his posts. They make video analysis on every breadcrumb so that anybody who is interested in learning about Q and his truths understands what is happening. They share these videos, blogs, and tweets on Facebook so that they can reach more people. The shares on social media are staggering. Conspiracy theory or not, nobody can deny that Q has touched and influenced millions of lives. And the person that Q may have helped the most is President Trump. Without Q's help, a lot of his supporters may have already given up on this seemingly clueless leader.

QANON AND HIS RELATIONSHIP WITH TRUMP

Just how close is Q to the president of the United States? Besides the picture proof of him riding in the airplane with the president, there are some other instances where Q seemed to be able to influence Trump.
For example, one Anon contacted Q and asked him to have the president use the phrase "tip top into one of Trump's many speeches. This was so that they can verify if Q indeed had pull on the leader and also to serve as a confirmation to the QAnon members that Trump is acknowledging them. Sure enough, in the president's address during a White House event, the Easter Egg Roll, Trump said that the White House is in "tippy top" shape.

It was also used in another speech that the president made where he was asking for "tip top" nuclear arsenal. After the speeches, Q posted the message that the request has been relayed to the president. He also asked if the QAnon readers listened to the president's speech. Coincidence? It could be but it still caused a lot of individuals to start believing that Q really had the president's ear.

Another well-analyzed instance where there seemed to be a connection with President Trump and QAnon was when Q posted several cryptic phrases, "Safety & Security" and "Catch & Release".

Afterward, President Trump posted a tweet on Twitter thanking the National Border Patrol Council's Brandon Judd for showing how badly the country needs the wall that he has been lobbying for from the very beginning of his administration.

The president included that measures must be taken in order to stop the loophole known as "catch & release" as well as clean up procedures of processes at the border for reasons of "safety & security". The use of the keywords released by Q was viewed by the QAnon members that Trump is indeed connected to Q and that he is secretly communication with them. Letting them know that he knows they are there. [10]

Another, albeit flimsy, example of Trump's covert acknowledgment that the QAnon movement exists was featured during one of his interview. There, he was talking about how he came to choose to become the US President. He mentioned that he visited Washington, D.C. about 17 times. The president repeated that statement several times. This number is significant to the followers of Q because the 17th letter of the alphabet just happens to be the letter Q. It was said that Trump was signaling the members that he knows they are out there.

If the posts of Q were indeed real, then this could indicate that the current administration has found an alternative channel by which they can communicate with their supporters, bypassing the traditional news outlets and even social media. This makes sense because Trump is not secretive of his dislike for mainstream media. He views them as the enemy. This channel is more direct. People think that if Trump has something to say to his supporters, he would need somebody like Q in order to reach them without alerting the people that are opposing him. Another point of legitimacy is that the administration has yet to confirm nor deny if the movement is indeed true. If it were not valid, the government would have spoken up by now in order to distance itself from a false channel. That is how many choose to justify the continuing existence of Q.

What the palace has done though is indirectly denounce groups that encourage others to do violent acts. This was established during an interview with Sara Huckabee Sanders, the White House press secretary, following the incident of hecklers harassing CNN's Jim Acosta. When she was asked whether the president supports the QAnon group, she simply stated that the president doesn't condone any group that will incite any form of violence against another individual. She added that the president definitely doesn't support any organization that supports and promote that type of behavior towards others.

While this may seem like a blow to QAnon, some individuals see this as encouraging. They claimed that the president is distancing himself from the group so that they can remain safe. If the public, and Deep State, knew that the president supports a group, its members could be put in danger. The followers believe that by publicly denouncing QAnon, the president is only protecting them. Still a lot of them believe that the president knows about the existence of the QAnon movement.

This is not the first time that government agencies have used alternative channels to send out communication. Back in the days of the first Cold War, the British and American spies would occasionally send coded messages placed in the classified ads of newspapers in order to talk to each other. The NSA was reported to be doing an updated version of this tactic.

Instead of using newspapers, they opted to utilize the groups public Twitter account in order to communicate with a potential source from Russia. This is just one small detail on this scandalous interaction. According to reports, CIA and NSA agents have traveled to Germany in order to try to recover certain pieces of cyberweapons that have been stolen from the intelligence agencies of America.

A spy from Russia supposedly offered the pilfered cyber tools back to the US in exchange for a whopping $10 million. The US agents eventually managed to have the price lowered to just a million dollars. The spy even offered up shocking information about President Trump. It was not determined whether the intelligence officers from the United States paid for the information that the spy was selling in addition to the cyber tools that was repurchased.

Based on the article, this unnamed Russian spy was able to meet in Germany with the US agents. In order to arrange the meeting and work out the details of their exchange, the NSA sent missives to the Russian spy using coded messages posted on their Twitter account. Some asked if the messages were sent directly or were, they posted in public.
According to James Risen, a writer from The Intercept, the messages were very much public. The tweet appeared completely benign but it contained hidden information that only the American and Russian spies understood. NSA has

reached out to various media channels to deny that it has been sending coded messages.

What is most troubling about this issue was not that the US intelligence agencies seemed keen on purchasing intelligence that could be bad for President Trump. This includes an alleged videotape of the president having relations with a sex worker recorded back in 2013. This will probably be met with indifference.

What is surprising is that these agencies have become so brazen that they are sending messages in plain sight. Their tweets are so public that no one would think to look further into what has been posted. No one except for the keen-eyed members of the QAnon movement.
Of course, when you are labeled a theorist, nobody would really pay attention to what you are saying, no matter how valid or true your message is.

Many individuals who have been keeping track of the social media posts of various government agencies have been labeled as theorists. This term is so dismissive that no matter what proof you present, nobody would believe you. Worse, these "theorists" are ridiculed and asked where their foil hats are. If a government agency tweets a certain date or a number, many theorists try to find connections to existing events. These get laughed at by most for being absurd. And then their paranoia gets vindicated when these types of revelations occur.

Many of the members of the QAnon movement are still waiting for their, "I told you so" moment. Once Q's prophecies finally come to fruition, these people will finally be "vindicated" for believing something that seemed so convolutedly harebrained. When the time comes, it is not just the QAnon followers who will win. They say that everybody wins because then, Deep State will be no more.

CHAPTER 2 – THE MOST POPULAR OF Q'S BREADCRUMBS

THE STORM – THE SECRET PLAN TO DECIMATE THE TOP MEMBERS OF THE DEEP STATE

December 5, 2018 was a special day that QAnon believers looked forward to. Many of them believed that the day will bring about a much sought-after justice against the world's biggest political enemies. It would be the completion of what they have been reading about since October of that year. What was that day? They believe it will be the beginning of the Storm.

What is it actually and how did that come to be? It was during what seemed like a typical Thursday night at the White House that the stirrings of The Storm began. This was back on October 5 of 2017. The members of the presidential press corps have just been told that they can go home. But at 7 p.m., they were called back to the State Dining Room. The president was holding a dinner for his military commanders and their spouses.

As the photographers and cameramen were taking photos and videos, the president suddenly gestured at the officials and said that this moment could be representing the "calm before the storm". Amidst the shouts of reporters asking him what his words meant, he said that he has the world's best military people inside the room and that they were all going to have a great evening. The press kept on asking him what he meant by The Storm but he simply told them that they will find out. Even a day after the event, upon being asked by different press members, the president simply says that they will eventually find out what he means.

Because he was with his country's military leaders, it was largely speculated that President Trump was alluding to an impending military operation. This was compounded by the fact that the group had their dinner right after the military officials discussed with the president the challenges that they had to take care of.

These were pertaining to the issues with North Korea, Afghanistan, Iran, ISIS, and the other revisionist powers that threaten the interests of the United States all over the world. During that meeting, Trump mentioned another challenge to North Korea, telling the members of the press who were present at that time, that the country will not allow the dictatorship of the leader to threaten the US nation as well as its allies. The president claimed that he and the country will do what is necessary in order to prevent any unimaginable loss in lives.

Additionally, during this gathering, Trump also claimed that the US is making tremendous progress regarding its fight against ISIS. He said that the media will find out about this progress in the coming days. He also said that the military is expected to provide him with a broad range of options. To what end, he didn't say. It is speculated by

QAnon followers that it has something to do with military actions probably against the countries mentioned earlier.

It could also have something to do with decertifying the nuclear agreement with Iran. Many were speculating whether The Storm has something to do with the international political chaos that this action will cause.

If this was the case, the plan was a highly secretive one because even his Vice President, Mike Pence, could not provide the press any answers regarding The Storm. Skeptics also mention that it could be nothing. This is not the first time that Trump mentioned something controversial and kept the press asking more questions.

Another popular interpretation by the bakers of QAnon sees this as the outpouring of the truth. The real truth though, according to QAnon, not some notion that has been prepared by entities with hidden agendas. What the QAnon followers, and other people, have discovered is that the truth can be controlled by whoever is releasing it. For this time, it is the mainstream media that controls the main bulk of what information gets released to the public.

While media is meant to be biased, it has been proven that they do, from time to time, color the kind of information that they serve to the public. Meaning, if the media wants the readers, listeners, and viewers to take information negatively, they can control what they print or broadcast in order to elicit that reaction from their audience. So, if mainstream media gets influenced by something or someone with the power to bend it to its will, it would be difficult for a regular person to tell if the information that has been released is true or it has been manufactured to elicit a certain reaction.

The "storm" could also be the action that people believe Donald Trump has been preparing for a long time – the release of thousands of indictments that should deal with top members of the cabal that the group has labeled as the Deep State. But before we go into the release of the storm of indictments, we have to go back and take a closer look at what issue started it all – Pizzagate.

It all begins with pizza and Anthony Weiner. On October 30 of 2016, an account on Twitter, specifically with the account name David Goldberg, started posting a claim that the NYPD (New York Police Department) was sifting through Anthony Weiner's computer and reading all his emails. We will recall that Anthony Weiner used to be a member of the US House of Representatives.

He was involved in a series of sex scandals that are related to sending text messages with a sexual nature. The scandal began when he was still a Congressman. He used Twitter to send links that yielded a picture of him in a sexually suggestive position. The receiver was a woman who as 21-year-old. During the investigation, it was discovered that the congressman has done this act multiple times but denies that he had any physical relationship with the women.

The politician had to take a break after that but returned to politics in 2013. This period was also riddled with accusations that he sexted three women, at the very least, after his resignation.

What prompted his arrest was when he sexted an

underaged girl in 2016. As part of the process, the FBI seized his laptop and accessed his emails. It was during this time that the Hillary Clinton email issue arose.

During the investigation on Weiner, FBI agents discovered several emails on his laptop that came from Huma Abedin. She was not only Anthony Weiner's wife; she was also the vice chair for Hillary Clinton's 2016 campaign for the presidential elections. The FBI believed that the electronic communication uncovered were relevant to an ongoing investigation on Clinton's server. [11]

According to another theory called the Pizzagate, the emails contained details that proved the existence of a huge network involved in pedophilia and the members of this were in the Democratic Party. Those with Internet access were also able to read and connect this with the leaked copies of emails from John Podesta's accounts back in 2016.

John Podesta was Hillary Clinton's campaign manager during that time. The account was hacked and copies of his electronic correspondence were posted on Wikileaks.

Wikileaks is a platform utilized for whistleblowing. It was founded by Julian Assange. According to him, the platform was established in order to acquire and disseminate data sets and documents that are classified in nature. Who obtains the information? Anonymous leakers.

It has been known to be an intelligence agency that is open source. A former employee, James Ball, claims that Wikileaks operates like the Government Communications Headquarters for the United Kingdom or the Central Intelligence Agency for the United States. However, the main difference is that Wikileaks gathers bits of intelligence

not for a specific country but for everyone.
Wikileaks has released thousands of military documents and over two hundred fifty thousand diplomatic cables. A couple of their leaks were said to have made a huge impact during the presidential election in 2016. It was the leak of emails from the Democratic National Committee and the emails of John Podesta that was seen as the final nail to the proverbial coffin for Clinton's campaign. [12]

One of Podesta's emails was highly scrutinized by the public. This was a missive to James Alefantis. Alefantis is the owner of a pizza place in D.C. - the Comet Ping Pong. In the email, Podesta brought up the possibility of Alefantis hosting a fundraiser for Hillary Clinton
The readers on 4Chan, after reading the copies of the emails began trying to put together a theory that connects Podesta and Alefantis. One theory grew to be what is now known as Pizzagate. It says that Comet Ping Pong is a headquarters of a group involved in child trafficking. Its leaders? Podesta and Clinton. Besides Clinton and Podesta, the ring involved individuals like George Soros, Barack Obama, James Comey, and more.

Many believed that some of the words that were used in the emails were code used in human trafficking and pedophilia. According to the people on 4Chan who interpreted Podesta's posted emails, every time the word "pizza" was mentioned, it was actually referring to pornography or pedophilia, depending on which source you'd like to believe. The same sources claimed that the word "pasta" was used to refer to a little boy. "Ice cream" was code for male prostitute. "Sauce" was really referring to an orgy.

It was in these posts that Comet Ping Pong was identified as the headquarters for this ring. It was also where Clinton and Huma allegedly brought the children which they kidnapped. More horrifically, it was said that it was at the store's basement that the children were tortured, sexually abused, and sacrificed to Satan. The claims also point at Clinton for using her political position to cover up these heinous acts.

According to other theorists, certain aspects of the Comet Ping Pong pizzeria were coded in order to covertly advertise the secret business to pedophiles. Its sign was said to be a symbol for Satanic rituals. [13]
The followers on Reddit and 4Chan also started looking into Alefantis' Instagram account. It was said that his account was filled with images of drugs, activities in gay clubs, and most disturbingly, of children. The followers commented that it was bizarre for Alefantis to be posting pictures of various children of different ages given that neither he nor his close associates did not appear to have any children.

This theory was originally posted on the Godlike Productions message board. It was then repeated on a post in Your News Wire. The theory was focused on Clinton bringing up old and disproven news run by NBC regarding allegations of sexual misconduct in the State Department. They said that she used her position as Secretary of State in order to help cover the entire thing up.

The hubbub regarding Pizzagate may have temporarily died down after several alleged violence related to it, but it certainly did not vanish.
On the afternoon of December 4, 2016, Edgar Maddison

Welch went inside Comet Ping Pong. He brought with him an assault rifle which he pointed at the employees of the pizzeria. Even though Welch fired his weapon inside the establishment, nobody got hurt. The employee that he pointed his rifle at was able to run outside and ask for assistance from the police.

After 45 minutes inside Comet Ping Pong, Welch emerged and surrendered to the police. He claimed that he was there in order to investigate if what he has been reading about the pizzeria is true. On his person, the police discovered a Colt .38 handgun, another shotgun, and a knife. According to Welch, he simply wanted to make sure if the things that he had been reading about the pizzeria is true.

Alefantis was quick to state that this was the evidence of how dangerous spreading fake news was. He claimed that while spreading malicious information may seem harmless, it could have terrible consequences. He also appealed to the public to stop "fanning the flames".

It was this, among a tide of complaints from readers, that prompted Reddit to ban posting on topics such as Pizzagate. [14]

This may have lessened the attack and threats to Alefantis and the employees of Comet Ping Pong. However, it was not the end to Pizzagate. To make the situation even more baffling, there were murmurings that the attack done by Welch may have been designed to discredit the theory.
In an unexpected turn, a Centipede Central moderator pointed out that Welch was once an actor. This lets more

than 6000 members of the chat room know that there is a possibility that Welch was hired in order to discredit and dissuade any more grassroots investigation with regards to this issue.

As proof to corroborate this idea, in the no-longer-existing subreddit on Pizzagate, it was posted that a traffic camera near the pizzeria has been moved one day before Welch went into Comet Ping Pong. This was very suspicious. Users began posting that the effort of Welch was just a false flag. [15]

With the banning of the Pizzagate subgroups on Reddit, the interest in Pizzagate idea went down significantly. Some people believed that the issue has been put to rest.

However, on the 28th of October in 2017, a cryptic message was posted on 4Chan's board called /pol/. User "BQ7V3bcW" posted that HRC was already being extradited. HRC is Hillary Rodham Clinton. The post claims that her passport has already been flagged and that they expect her to try to run to another country. Additionally, the post warns the readers that massive riots could ensue, organized by the group led by Clinton, in order to show defiance to this act. The post also expected personalities to start fleeing the country to avoid being arrested as well.

The post continues by saying that the US Marshalls will be the one to conduct the operation while the National Coastguard has already been activated. The anonymous poster even provides a way to check the validity of the post by telling the reader to call on any coast guard from any major city and ask whether they are activated for duty on

October 30.

This post sparked a re-examination of the old ideas posed by Pizzagate. People immediately assumed that Clinton was finally being arrested for her part in running the alleged sex trafficking ring. This time, the post had a more widespread reach. The poster, QAnon, had a stronger following. Individuals kept mentioning this post on their Twitter and Facebook accounts. Some even started dedicated YouTube Channels just to discuss and analyze online QAnon's post. Among those who shared the messages of Q was the Jaselskis.

On January 23 at around 8:07 p.m., Chrissy and Paul Jaselskis posted an entry on YouTube entitles "Melissa Video". This video alleges that the world is run by a satanic pedophile group who is composed of the most influential people in the world, including politicians and Hollywood celebrities.

At 9:17 pm of the same day, Ryan was said to have gone into Comet Ping Pong and started a fire. The fire was not that big though. It was already extinguished by the time the firefighters arrived. It was not immediately clear who started the fire and whether it was intentional. The employees of the pizzeria, however, claimed that they already called the police that day because they have been receiving highly suspicious "prank calls". When the authorities investigated, they found out that Ryan Jaselskis, whose identity was unknown then, intentionally left baby food and a diaper inside the restaurant. An apparent nod to the claim that the pizzeria was a hub for pedophiles.

One week after, the authorities released a video showing a man that was thought to have started the fire inside

Comet Ping Pong. Nearly two weeks after, Jaselskis was confronted by the police, not for the arson, for jumping the fence at the Washington Monument. After a scuffle with the authorities, Jaselskis finally gave up and was arrested.
Days after, he was linked to the Comet Ping Pong arson case when the jacket that he was wearing during his arrest was discovered to be the same jacket that the arson was wearing on the video. He was then charged for property damage and is held without bond. [16]

The kicker in this story is that, just like Welch, Ryan Jaselskis was also a fledgling actor. His IMDb profile picture also featured him wearing the same jacket as the one that implicated him in the fire. This is why there are so many questions regarding his involvement. Was he really prompted by the discoveries and posts of QAnon? Was he hired to put to bed any more questions regarding the connection between Clinton, Alefantis, and Comet Ping Pong? [17]

Because a lot of people who were aware of the Pizzagate issue were disgusted with what could be happening under their noses, they waited in anticipation to see what the investigation will lead to. They waited for the first blow that Donald Trump will give this child sex ring group. Unfortunately, October 30, 2017, came and went with no indictment being released.

To explain the apparent non-arrest of Clinton despite being promised a "Storm", Q followers believed that instead of being extradited, she was collared in secret and is now being tracked by the authorities with the use of an ankle bracelet. Dozens of pictures of Hillary Clinton posted online are being analyzed by QAnon followers to see if her outfits are specifically chosen to hide the tracking device. [18]

In November of 2017, the buzz about this ankle bracelet reached its peak. This was when Hillary Clinton and Senator John McCain started wearing walkable boots. The two had very different reasons for wearing the said contraption. For Clinton, it was allegedly due to an unfortunate accident that left her with a broken toe. As for McCain, it was said that he had to wear the boot after going through surgery from a tear to the Achilles tendon. However, several followers of Q claimed that these were just excuses to hide their ankle bracelets. They said that the two have already been arrested and the ankle bracelets were placed so that they cannot leave the country. The rumor was further intensified by the fact the McCain apparently wore his surgical boots on the wrong foot two weeks after. On several photos, the senator wore the boot on his left leg.

December 5 is another important day for QAnon followers. Trump's shutdown of several executive departments plus the closure of the stock exchange were viewed by the followers, not as a memorial or tribute to George W. Bush's death but rather a prelude to the storm - the mass arrest that was long promised by Q. They said that Trump timed the closure of the stock market to coincide with this event in order to head off possible chaos that would ensue.

QAnon members were vigilant of any signs that would signal the beginning of the storm. Even the position of Bush's coffin was said to be lying on a Q-shaped pattern on the floor. Because the movement considered Bush as a criminal president, his coffin was so placed to serve as a warning to the Deep State. They even thought that the letter "D" and a number "5" posted on the windows of a bus that was there during Bush's funeral is a sign that this was the vehicle that was going to be used to transport the Anti-Trump ring members to Guantanamo.

To the disappointment of many, the mass arrest did not happen. However, it was not a complete failure, according to QAnon members. It was just to lull the enemy into complacency. The plan is still in place, Trump is just still waiting for the right moment to begin taking his steps for the draining of the so-called swamp.

THE STORY OF THE MOCKINGBIRD

On the same day that QAnon posted about Hillary Clinton's supposed indictment, another message was posted on the 4Chan /pol/ board by the same user.

There are so many names mentioned. There's HRC which refers to Hillary Rodham Clinton. She is featured in a lot of posts and notions pushed forward by the movement. The post also mentions Barack Obama, Huma Abedin, and George Soros.

But at the top of the post is a word that has thousands of followers confused. "Mockingbird" was that word. In succeeding QAnon posts and the entries of the movement's bakers, this term is often repeated. The term, as many believe, refers to Operation Mockingbird, a project allegedly funded by the CIA. It was created in order to manipulate the news media outfits for propaganda purposes.

Based on reports made by Deborah Davis, the group from this project recruited top American journalists and made them part of the propaganda network. They also oversaw the operations of various student and cultural organizations that served as the project's front.

The CIA's support for these groups was exposed when the 1967 issue of the Ramparts magazine revealed that the CIA gave funding for the National Student Association. A succeeding congressional investigation also exposed that the Agency also funded various civics and journalist groups. At this time though, the project's name was never mentioned in any reports.

The name Project Mockingbird was first mentioned in the report titled CIA Family Jewels compiled at around 1970. In 2007, a declassified version of this report came out. It yielded information that the CIA wire-tapped two journalists from the US during the early 1960s. This activity went on for several months.

It was also discovered that this type of activity already happened in the early 1950s. Towards the beginning of the Cold War, there were many efforts made by the US and the Soviet Union to use media outlets to intentionally influence public opinion. The Communist group established a front called the International Organization of Journalists. The organization received funding from Moscow and controlled every reporter on all major newspaper companies in Europe. They made sure that only stories that promoted the Communist cause would get out. [19]

As an answer to the propaganda started by the Soviet Union, director Frank Wisner of the Office of Policy Coordination set up Operation Mockingbird. He recruited the co-owner of The Washington Post, Phil Graham, to help him run the project. At around 1951, Wisner was able to coerce or influence respected press members from CBS, Newsweek, The New York Times, as well as other communication companies. It was at this time that Cord

Meyer came to become the principal operative of Operation Mockingbird.

By 1953, the project was able to control 25 wire agencies and newspapers. Under the directorship of Allen Dulles, these media network released reports that were carefully developed using CIA-provided information. This intelligence will then be picked up by other reporters and spread all over the rest of the media wire services.

The discovery of the activities of Operation Mockingbird was brought about by the investigation conducted by the U.S. Congress right after the Watergate Scandal. Concerned that the president may have abused his authority over the CIA, they had several entities look into the activities conducted by the agency. In 1975, Seymour Hersh, an investigative journalist, published an expose that exposed the agency's ties to numerous private organizations and journalists. The project name was still not unearthed.

In 1976, a more thorough report on the CIA's activities yielded the agency's connection with both domestic and foreign media outlets. It stated that the Central Intelligence Agency maintains relationships with more than a hundred individuals all over the world. They not only provide the agency with intelligence; they also influence the opinions of the masses using covert propaganda.

These individuals hold control of a large number of periodicals and newspapers. They also have ties with companies that own television and radio stations, as well as book publishers. As for their ties on US soil, about fifty of the CIA's assets were journalists or members of various media organizations.

According to the CIA, as early as 1976, the agency was already trying to limit its clandestine utilization of journalists. At the end of 1976, the CIA allegedly already cut ties with its media contacts. However, some freelancers were said to not have been decommissioned.

In 2007, the name Project Mockingbird finally came into light. As mentioned, the details were part of the declassified report requested by James R. Schlesinger, then CIA's director.

Based on this report, the project was a telephone intercept kind. It was done from March 12, 1963, until June 15 of the same year. Its target was two newsmen who were publishing articles based on intelligence coming from the agency itself. Most of the information was classified.

The surveillance was authorized by John McCone, a CIA director. He did this in coordination with Robert Kennedy, Robert McNamara, and Joseph Carroll. These were all high-ranking officials of the government.

One of those two newsmen was a syndicated columnist named Paul Scott. His son, Jim Scott, recalls that they thought his father was going crazy. He said that his father would worry so much about the government wiretapping his phone that he would often go to their neighbor's home to make important calls. After 45 years, upon the declassification of the CIA's family jewels that they found out that his father's seeming paranoia was justified. [20]

This entire activity is the reason why QAnon and the movement have labeled mainstream media as their enemy.

If it happened before, who is to say that it is not happening again now? Whenever there is a particular report that goes against what Q posted, they dismiss it as part of the continuing effort of the CIA to control the information that is being released to the public through news outlets.

QAnon has warned the movement's followers that they can no longer trust the information that is being fed to them. They have to rely on Q as well as the president for clues as to what is really happening. This is part of the Great Awakening that is being talked about. This is also why, according to Q, the president is bypassing the CIA and surrounding himself with generals. He is allegedly doing that so he cannot be influenced by those who belong to the Deep State and their puppeteers.

DEEP STATE'S PUPPET MASTERS – SOROS, ROTHSCHILD, AND HOUSE OF SAUD

By now, you may have heard of or read about Deep State several times. What is this mysterious entity that everybody is blaming for all the bad things that are happening in the world? When people learn that the Muslim Brotherhood blew up another building, they think it was backed by Deep State.

If there is an existing child sex trafficking case, it was caused by Deep State. The existence of the Internet? That was created by the Deep State so that they can keep control of the information that gets out to the people. What is Deep State and why are they hell-bent on keeping people poor and misinformed?

QAnon believers have varying views of what Deep State is. For some, it is a dark cabal of highly powerful individuals who get to stay rich and influential only if they keep people ignorant. If there is war in one country, people will not have the time nor the energy to look closer on the motivation of their leaders. If there is a plague, people will be too busy getting sick or panicking to avoid becoming sick in order to oppose the people who are benefiting from the illness. Those people who cause war, famine, and chaos are the puppet masters of the Deep State.

Other members of QAnon believe that Deep State is those people who used to be influential but are no longer in power. They still have enough pull to cause huge problems for the current administration. These are the real enemies of Trump. They undermine his authority and make it more difficult for him to pass anything that they view to make the country great again.

There are a few developments within the country that give followers a clue on just how brutal the battle is between Deep State and the president. One of the incidents cited by QAnon and the bakers is the one that took place on April 9 of 2018. The FBI raided the hotel room and office of Michael Cohen. Cohen is Trump's personal attorney. Trump was quick to come this attorney's defense, calling the raid a witch hunt. That same day, Trump was visited by 20 of his military leaders.

QAnon bakers cite this as the military's show of support for the Head of State. More significantly, they were photographed with the president with nine officials on his right and eleven more to his left. This, the bakers claimed, was a reference to the 9/11 attack that was allegedly known to the military as a false flag attack masterminded by the Deep State. This show of military support is said to be proof that the military has chosen a side – Trump's.

As mentioned in the many QAnon posts, Trump has been chosen by a group, composed mainly of military officials, to expose and put an end to the Deep State. This group has been working hard to keep Deep State from derailing their plans, including their efforts to prevent the president from being inaugurated after Trump's surprise victory in 2016.

QAnon claimed that the attack on Cohen was just another if a more escalated, effort to destabilize the current administration. Q's bakers believe that the raid was conducted in order to find some "dirt" on Trump and his businesses. These will be used by the Deep State eventually as bullets for the president.

The QAnon believers claim that this raid came less than a day after a chemical weapons attack occurred in Syria. This supposed false flag attack was pinned on the Assad regime. Deep State was said to be manipulating the US president to attack Syria. However, it is also said that Trump saw through Deep State's machination and limited the missile strike that was conducted on April 14.

This was a carefully orchestrated plan to avoid any direct confrontation with the Russian forces but enough to fool Deep State into thinking that they had the upper hand. It was said that even President Putin of Russia knew of Trump's plan which is why he did not order any retaliation on the US military forces that conducted the air strike.

Many may be wondering who Deep State is. If you look at the posts of QAnon and his followers, you will notice that they are pointing to three entities that are pulling the strings within this group: George Soros, The House of Saud, and the Rothschild family. What is Q's proof? He claims that you need to follow the trail of money to find out.

On the 11th of November in 2017, QAnon posted an entry on 4Chan. It posed several questions to his believers.

Starting with the oldest of the three masters, the Rothschilds is said to be one of the richest and most influential families in the world. Their influence reaches back to when the Napoleonic war took place. The Rothschilds owe their vast wealth to intelligent lending of money to the British Empire as well as other Monarchial adversaries of Napoleon. The family's wealth grew exponentially after the defeat of Napoleon.

It was not just money that the Rothschild amassed during that period, they were also rewarded aristocratic titles and national honors by the monarchs that they lent money to. This pushed the members of the Rothschild family to prominence all throughout the nineteenth century.

According to QAnon, the total cumulative wealth of this particular family is way above the current estimates being posted. He claims that their true wealth could be closer to $2 trillion. Given this unimaginable wealth, it is not difficult to imagine what and who they can buy in order to influence the world into doing and thinking what they want to world to do or believe. They could be funding wars, causing environmental issues, and any other depravities that keep the rest of the world in the dark.

Another influential family that QAnon wants his followers to keep their eyes on are the members of the House of Saud. While media pegged this family's wealth at $1.4 trillion, Q estimates that it should be closer to $4 trillion. Given the number of members of this family, as well as their various holdings in different industries, it is more likely that QAnon's estimate is closer than what the media researchers have released.

Finally, we take a look at the wealth amassed by George Soros. He is a very prominent hedge fund manager whose total assets is pegged at $24 billion. Again, QAnon believes that this is a very low estimate. He claimed that it should be closer to $1 trillion.

So, what do these entities do with all that wealth? Based on QAnon's post, they wield their wealth in order to control the national elites and politicians worldwide.

In one of QAnon's post, it was mentioned that the Rothschild were cult leaders and has significant influence over the church. Where is this notion rooted? It is known that in 1832, the Vatican borrowed money from this family, making the church heavily indebted influence-wise on the Rothschilds. This influence is said to have corrupted the church from then on. [21]

Additionally, this family possesses a controlling interest in a network of private and central banks. This gives them enormous influence all over the world. In turn, politicians in any part of the can be manipulated through financial means. The Rothschilds can choose which personality to put into office through financial aids in that person's campaigns. Subsequently, once that person is in office, he or she is definitely in the family's pockets, influencing whatever action is done to that politician's capacity.

QAnon proves this claim via the revelation of Dr. Bill

Deagle. Deagle was a physician that worked at the US Space Command. He claims that he was inexplicably approached by Guy de Rothschild. He said that Rothschild introduced himself as the "Pindar" or the CEO of the entire Earth and displayed unimaginable occult powers.

In the same QAnon post, he referred to SA or Saudi Arabia as a major player in oil technology, hold influence on politicians both in the UK and the US, and control over major technology companies. More disturbingly, he connects Saudi Arabia to the issue of sex trafficking of children. QAnon claims that these claims are not surprising as the House of Saud has maintained control of oil reserves from many decades.

On November 4, Q started talking about SA. This refers to Saudi Arabia, or more specifically, the House of Saud, the ruling family of the said country.

It is in these posts that QAnon started using the signature Alice AND Wonderland. The anons worked hard to decode this signature and made sure to mention that it was not "in" just like the title of Lewis Carroll's book but "and". Eventually, it was found that Alice refers to Hillary Clinton. Wonderland was Saudi Arabia. This is connected to QAnon's other signature – White Rabbit.

For the longest time, Saudi Arabia has been blatantly disregarding international laws. For example, in 2013, the country violently executed a total of 79 people. In 2015, a total of a hundred and fifty people were beheaded. It is obvious that the people running Riyadh think themselves to be above the prophet, the Righteous Caliphs, and even the words of their holy book. They have been seeking religious ways to justify their violent punishments. This is why the country was labeled as The Bloody Wonderland. Clinton was obviously getting funding from this country. But why? Because she is key to covering up many illegal activities not only in the US but also in that particular region. She is also said to be the primary mover in a global child trafficking ring that is linked to the said House and to other major families in the world.

With that wealth, it is easy to control leaders of countries using outright bribery or through campaign contributions. QAnon substantiates the level of influence that the House of Saud has on the politicians using the September 11 attacks. He says that sixteen out of the nineteen hijackers were identified to be Saudi citizens. Who do the US army and NATO allies attack? Afghanistan.

In the 9/11 Commission Report that was authorized by the US Congress, the involvement of Saudi was hidden by classifying a huge chunk of the report. It was only in 2016 that the hidden pages of the report were revealed. This exposed the participation of Saudi Arabia's Ambassador to the US, Prince Bandar, who allegedly provided money for at least a couple of the hijackers. The release of this declassified report led to the arrest of Prince Bandar, other prominent Royal Family members, as well as several senior officials of Saudi. This, according to QAnon, was part of the "Draining the Swamp" process that Trump is enacting.

Finally, we go back to George Soros who was able to raise his value to approximately $1 trillion by betting against the British Pound way back in 1992. Based on the posts by QAnon, Soros is the one responsible for shaping the public opinion to favor the Deep State. He does this using his Open Society Foundation. He is said to have been covertly funding political opponents and dissidents that have tumbled numerous political regimes.

He was also said to have been a major mover in the domestic opposition of Trump's election. He allegedly directed funds towards progressive organizations that favor the agenda of the Deep State. This activity was revealed in 2017 when an investigation was conducted by Jeff Sessions, with the Department of Justice. According to the report, slush funds were being diverted to organizations that work to oppose the current administration. [22]

Another notable connection is between Soros and the judge that was selected to oversee Michael Cohen's case. US District Judge Kimba Wood. Wood was also the one who officiated the wedding of Soros back in 2013. This tie with Soros shows how people that are close to the hedge fund manager gets appointed to important positions in order to serve as stumbling blocks for Trump.

QAnon posted an entry back on February 5th of 2018 claiming that it was Soros who compromised the Clintons. However, he also claimed that the evil really entered their system only after they associated themselves with the Rothschilds. It was under their influence that Bill Clinton visited Epstein's island frequently.

Epstein's island is a private Caribbean island that is owned by billionaire recluse, Jeffrey Epstein. It was said to be a venue for satanic rituals as well as the place where politicians and Hollywood personalities abuse and sacrifice children in the most depraved ways. Jeffrey Epstein himself was said to be a pedophile, accused of enlisting underage females into his sex-slave network. It was said that he evaded arrest for so long by paying off his victims. [23]

Epstein, despite being bombarded by accusations of abuse against young women, has managed to avoid major consequences to his crime due to his connections and wealth. His wealth enabled him to assemble a team that was able to pay off or intimidate victims and prevented them from coming forward. Epstein also became a key witness against executives of Bear Stearns, which helped him avoid a substantial prison sentence. [24]

Given the substantial influence, either through cooperation or coercion, and wealth of these puppet masters, it is unimaginable what they can do. They can place people in power, remove enemies from their path, have crimes go away, start wars, and coerce countries into making policies that favor them. Which is why QAnon wants his followers to keep an eye on these entities. Every time something huge takes place, he cautions them to be vigilant and find the connection. Because there is a huge chance that there is a connection.

Is Kim Jong-un of North Korea a CIA puppet?

Continuing with the influence of the three major Deep State masters, one notion that QAnon is mentioning is Deep State's control over North Korea. The Triangle - Rothschild family, House of Saud, and Soros – want to keep the entire world at the brink of a nuclear apocalypse. This makes sense because what will make a nation remain docile and obedient more than the threat of being nuked.

For this threat to seem like a reality, the Triangle required a scapegoat. They needed to control a country that has a military nuclear weapons program. The best one of the countries with that type of weaponry is North Korea. Besides its nukes, North Korea also possesses biological and chemical weapons. The country is also not a party to the NPT or Non-Proliferation of Nuclear Weapons. In fact, it has been sanctioned several times for conducting nuclear testing.

So, it is said that Deep State formed a new nation and positioned a puppet leader who can easily be manipulated in order to keep the nuclear threat alive. According to QAnon's bakers, it was the CIA that had a hand in placing the Kim family in power.

It was recently that Trump has tried to reach out to Kim Jong-un and begin the process of having him denuclearize North Korea. Just before the two leaders held their 2018 summit, QAnon posted about a deal being made between the two.

Q also mentioned that the Clown was out. According to numerous bakers, the "Clown" refers to the CIA. Q claimed that the talks between Trump and King Jong-un lead to the "strings" being cut, or the influence finally ending. It was made clear that Kim and Trump already had a denuclearization pact as early as 2017 when Trump first had his Asian trip. Q also mentioned that the Singapore summit was actually just a ploy to keep Deep State confused.

The second meeting between Trump and Kim, the two leaders were supposed to hammer out an understanding to reunify Korea. However, unlike the first meeting, this was not a success. QAnon mentioned that Trump was intent on making this new deal that he was willing to risk going back to Asia despite having survived an assassination attempt.
What assassination attempt, you might ask? And why was this not reported by any major news outlet?

It was in the early hours on June 10 when a webcam that has been set up to take a video of Puget Sound, in the vicinity of Whidbey Island in Washington, caught on video what looked like a missile being fired.

The owner of the webcam immediately posted what his camera has captured. The more observant of the QAnon members immediately realized that not only was there a missile launched, but it was also obviously directed to take down the Air Force One, which was then on its way to Singapore, transporting the president towards his fateful meeting with Kim Jong-un. [25]

Doubters claim that this was not a missile but rather a lens flare that was captured by the webcam. This is based on the statement of the camera owner that his camera captures one image every forty seconds and each shot has a 20 second exposure time.

Still more believe that it was a missile as Whidbey Island has a naval base. Additionally, there are other bases in the area. More significantly, there is a nuclear submarines base in Bangor, just 60 miles south of where the alleged missile appeared. Researchers claimed that the missile could not have been launched from Whidbey as the base situated there has no missile launchers.

So, it is more likely that the missile came from a submarine. However, skeptics also mentioned that there is a reason by the Navy never tests any weapon in Puget Sound. This is because the area is heavily populated. To top that off, judging from the photo, the missile was really high in the sky and was directed straight up.

Experts claim that no submarine has the capacity to do that nor shoot down a fast-moving aircraft at that angle. It was also determined that the picture was the only proof that any missile was launched. People residing in the area did not report seeing, or at the very least hearing, a missile being launched.

There was also no debris found in the area. Of course, this

doesn't mean that there really is no missile launched in an attempt to assassinate Trump. Who knows what kind of advanced military weapons the Triangle has funded in order to prevent Trump from undoing their plans? It is widely known that Deep State will not stop at anything in order to get what they want. QAnon members even claim that they are behind the murder of Seth Rich.

THE PLOT TO MURDER SETH RICH

Seth Rich was an employee of the Democratic National Committee (DNC). At around 4:20 am on July 10 of 2016, he was shot in the back while walking in the Bloomingdale neighborhood in Washington. The police went to the scene after hearing gunshots. They found Rich still conscious and they were able to bring him to the hospital. Unfortunately, Rich succumbed to his injuries less than an hour later. Authorities believed that he was a victim of an attempted robbery that had gone awry.

Speculations about this untimely death began flying when it was revealed by an investigator, Rod Wheeler, that Rich contacted the people running WikiLeaks right before his death. Wheeler claimed that there were emails that supported this.

QAnon members believe that Seth Rich was murdered as retaliation for being part of the email leak in DNC. It is notable that this leak resulted in an investigation of the Clinton Foundation. The Metropolitan Police Department has claimed that Wheeler's findings were unfounded. Mr. Wheeler himself, during an interview with CNN, admitted that he found no proof to support his statements.

During the investigation, it was said that the intelligence agency in Russia tried to implicate Seth Rich as the main source of the stolen information from DNC in order to direct attention away from them. Time zones and date stamps were altered in order to make it appear that the intelligence that was obtained was accessed a mere five days before Rich was shot. However, based on the report presented by Mueller, the email containing the email files that were sent to WikiLeaks arrived four days after Rich died.

A month after this report, Julian Assange, the founder, and owner of WikiLeaks hinted that Rich's death could be connected to the fact that he shared some information with WikiLeaks. According to Assange, their whistle-blowers go through significant risks and put in a huge effort just to get information to them.

He didn't out rightly claim that he was referring to Seth Rich but merely said that a 27-year old informant who worked for DNC was murdered, shot in back, in a street in Washington. When pressed by the reporter of the Dutch television network that was interviewing him, Assange still refused to mention any name. He simply warned his sources that they be aware of the risks that they will be taking should they choose to become a whistle-blower. WikiLeaks also offered a significant reward amounting to $20,000 for any relevant information about the death of Seth Rich.

Officials of the America intelligence released an intelligence report stating that they believe WikiLeaks was granted access by the Russian military intelligence to stolen DNC material. This was done in order to influence the presidential election. Assange vehemently denied this accusation. It must have been somebody between those two parties that was trying to pin the leak on Rich in order to cover up for this.

QAnon believers still do not buy the botched robbery angle presented by the police because, while his watch strap got damaged in the incident, his possessions, including his wallet, were still on him when he was found. This strengthens the notion that Rich could have been murdered for other, more sinister, reasons. [26]

THE REAL OBJECTIVE OF THE MUELLER INVESTIGATION

People, both QAnon followers, and skeptics, impatiently waited for the release of the contents of the Mueller's report. This report is a result of a comprehensive investigation regarding the involvement of the Russians in the presidential election back in 2016. Many already know some of the contents of this report because there have been so many incidences of intelligence leakage from the US Congress.

However, most QAnon believers were still hoping that the report will reveal what QAnon has been telling them about for months – that Mueller was not really looking into Trump and his possible collusion with the Russians. Rather, Mueller was taking this opportunity to uncover the involvement of Hillary Clinton and other personalities in a global child predator ring.

In July of 2016, the Federal Bureau of Investigation began looking into the possible link between the associates of Trump and the officials from Russia. This was brought about by the information on Trump's campaign that was forwarded to the FBI by George Papadopoulos, a foreign policy adviser. This inquiry was led by James Comey who was then the Director of the FBI. In May of 2017, President Trump suddenly decided to dismiss Comey.

More than 130 lawmakers from the Democratic party called for the appointment of a special counsel as a response to the firing of Comey. Eight days after the said firing, the new FBI Director, Andrew McCabe, opened another investigation to find out if Trump committed an obstruction of justice for reasons including the dismissal of Comey.

It was also at that time that Rod Rosenstein, Deputy Attorney General, assigned Robert Mueller as special counsel. He was to take over the existing counterintelligence investigation. Additionally, he was in charge of looking into whether trump obstructed justice in the case of Comey. The scope of Mueller's investigation included allegations of coordination between the presidential campaign of Trump and the government of Russia. He was also given the authority to prosecute any individual who attempted to interfere with his investigation.

The investigation took almost two years from May 17 of 2017 until March 22 of 2019. It resulted in thirty-four indictments against a number of previous members of the Trump campaign. The investigation was so comprehensive that it took about 500 search warrants and about 500 witnesses were interviewed. It cost over $25 million to conclude.

After all that time, the report was finally submitted to William Barr, the Attorney General. His office, in turn, created a four-page summary of the conclusions made in the report. While there were many individuals indicted, the report did not find sufficient evidence to prove that Trump and his team conspired with Russia to sway the outcome of the presidential election.

Trump's ex-campaign chairman, Paul Manafort, and Richard Gates were both charged conspiracy to launder money, tax evasion, providing false statements, conspiracy against the US, and many more. Michael Flynn, the former national security adviser, was also charged for lying to the FBI regarding his conversations with a certain Russian ambassador.

Michael Cohen, the former personal attorney of Trump, also pleaded guilty of making false statements regarding projects in Russia. It was claimed that this was done in order to minimize the link between Trump and the Moscow Project. While there were so many indictments, the Justice Department claimed that none of these crimes actually had an impact on the outcome of the presidential election. [27]

While Trump cooperated with the investigation, he called it out for being an illegal takedown. He also claimed that the result of the report completely exonerated him from all the allegations that were leveled against him.

Many QAnon followers were disappointed because none of the report's conclusions had anything to do with Deep State or with the indictment of Hillary Clinton. However, QAnon was quick to defend this by claiming that Trump is sitting on the findings and is waiting for the perfect moment to take down the cabal.

Q reminded the members that the "draining" of the swamp which is the US government is a long game for Trump and he is not in a hurry to strike knowing that the enemies are very strong. He has to wait for the most opportune moment to unleash what the Mueller report has truly unearthed.

People, both QAnon followers, and skeptics, impatiently waited for the release of the contents of the Mueller's report. This report is a result of a comprehensive investigation regarding the involvement of the Russians in the presidential election back in 2016. Many already know some of the contents of this report because there have been so many incidences of intelligence leakage from the US Congress.

However, most QAnon believers were still hoping that the report will reveal what QAnon has been telling them about for months – that Mueller was not really looking into Trump and his possible collusion with the Russians. Rather, Mueller was taking this opportunity to uncover the involvement of Hillary Clinton and other personalities in a global child predator ring.

In July of 2016, the Federal Bureau of Investigation began looking into the possible link between the associates of Trump and the officials from Russia. This was brought about by the information on Trump's campaign that was forwarded to the FBI by George Papadopoulos, a foreign policy adviser. This inquiry was led by James Comey who was then the Director of the FBI. In May of 2017, President Trump suddenly decided to dismiss Comey.

More than 130 lawmakers from the Democratic party called for the appointment of a special counsel as a response to the firing of Comey. Eight days after the said firing, the new FBI Director, Andrew McCabe, opened another investigation to find out if Trump committed an obstruction of justice for reasons including the dismissal of Comey.

It was also at that time that Rod Rosenstein, Deputy Attorney General, assigned Robert Mueller as special counsel. He was to take over the existing counterintelligence investigation. Additionally, he was in charge of looking into whether Trump obstructed justice in the case of Comey. The scope of Mueller's investigation included allegations of coordination between the presidential campaign of Trump and the government of Russia. He was also given the authority to prosecute any individual who attempted to interfere with his investigation.

The investigation took almost two years from May 17 of 2017 until March 22 of 2019. It resulted in thirty-four indictments against a number of previous members of the Trump campaign. The investigation was so comprehensive that it took about 500 search warrants and about 500 witnesses were interviewed. It cost over $25 million to conclude.

After all that time, the report was finally submitted to William Barr, the Attorney General. His office, in turn, created a four-page summary of the conclusions made in the report. While there were many individuals indicted, the report did not find sufficient evidence to prove that Trump and his team conspired with Russia to sway the outcome of the presidential election.

Trump's ex-campaign chairman, Paul Manafort, and Richard Gates were both charged conspiracy to launder money, tax evasion, providing false statements, conspiracy against the US, and many more. Michael Flynn, a former national security adviser, was also charged for lying to the FBI regarding his conversations with a certain Russian ambassador.

Michael Cohen, the former personal attorney of Trump, also pleaded guilty of making false statements regarding projects in Russia. It was claimed that this was done in order to minimize the link between Trump and the Moscow Project. While there were so many indictments, the Justice Department claimed that none of these crimes actually had an impact on the outcome of the presidential election.

Mueller also indicted thirteen citizens from Russia, as well as three Russian entities. The latter included the Internet Research Agency. He also added an indictment of Konstantin Kilimnik. Kilimnik is a business partner of Paul Manafort. It was found out that Manafort passed on internal data related to campaign polling to Kilimnik.

In July of the same year, a dozen members of Fancy Bear, a cyber espionage group from Russia have been indicted as well. Fancy Bear was responsible for the DNC email hacking incident in 2016. In 2019, Roger Stone, a long-time advisor to Trump was indicted on a total of seven charges.

While Trump cooperated with the investigation, he called it out for being an illegal takedown. He also claimed that the result of the report completely exonerated him from all the allegations that were leveled against him.

In the beginning, Pro-Trump parties were worried about what the result of the Special Counsel investigation will yield. Of course, there could be collusion within the investigating body that can come up with made-up documents that can implicate President Trump. They were reassured by Q that nothing of that sort will happen.

According to breadcrumbs dropped by Q, the investigation is not corrupt. He also claimed that Robert Mueller was conducting this investigation not against Trump but against the people who are members of the Deep State, namely Clinton and Obama. It was said that Trump and Mueller agreed that the investigation had to appear to go after Trump so that the real targets will lower their guards.

Q noted that there are over a thousand sealed indictments that are waiting to be executed. In other reports, it said that there were 25,000 of those sealed indictments. The release of them is known as "draining the swamp".

Many QAnon followers were disappointed because none of the report's conclusions had anything to do with Deep State or with the indictment of Hillary Clinton. However, QAnon was quick to defend this by claiming that Trump is sitting on the findings and is waiting for the perfect moment to take down the cabal.

Q reminded the members that the "draining" of the swamp which is the US government is a long game for Trump and he is not in a hurry to strike knowing that the enemies are very strong. He has to wait for the most opportune moment to unleash what the Mueller report has truly unearthed.

THE SINKING OF THE TITANIC – HOW J.P. MORGAN GOT RID OF HIS RIVALS

In the evening of April 14 in the year 1912, the "unsinkable" R.M.S. Titanic hit a huge iceberg and sank into the North Atlantic. 1,503 unlucky individuals of the total 2,223 passengers sank with the ship. This seemingly random disaster rocked the world and hundreds of theories were born to try to explain how the impossible happened that fateful night.

According to one story, J.P. Morgan, a then millionaire banker, masterminded the sinking of the Titanic during its tragic maiden voyage because his rivals were on board. The rivals were other millionaires Isidor Straus, Benjamin Guggenheim, and Jacob Astor. Isidor Straus was also a banker and the owner of the Macy's department store. Benjamin Guggenheim owned a manufacturing company that made mining machinery. Jacob Astor was a renowned builder of skyscrapers and buildings. All three perished that night.

Surprisingly, J. Pierpont Morgan was supposed to be on the ship too. He planned to go to America via the Titanic.

However, the millionaire had to forfeit his spot at the last minute and had to stay abroad a little bit longer. During this time, Morgan was trying to transport his extensive art collection to New York. It would be traveling by sea from England to France. Then from the French soil, it would make its way to New York where it would be housed at the Metropolitan Museum of Art.

However, the banker was not able to meet the art specialist sent to London by the US Customs Office. The officer had to leave for the States unexpectedly. Morgan had to reschedule his meeting with the art specialist for mid-April of that year. This inopportune event forced him to stay in Southampton, England. Was one of the world's richest men also one of the luckiest? Not according to Q.

Some say Morgan wanted to get rid of the competition while others believed that the reason why they were offed was that Straus, Guggenheim, and Astor were opposed to the conception of the Federal Reserve. [28]

How was Morgan able to do this? It was discovered that the company that built the ship and operated it on its trip was White Star Line. This was owned by International Mercantile Marine. Who owns this? You are right. J.P. Morgan. Some say that Morgan made sure that the ship was equipped with the wrong signal flares. Some also claimed that the deck of the Titanic could be sealed shut using electromagnets. It was this that closed all the exits and trapped the passengers.

Another version of the theory claims that, instead of J.P. Morgan, it was another banking family that caused the sinking of the Titanic. This family was the Rothschild. This influential family founded many banking houses all over

Europe in the 1800s and have been a favorite target for unproven theories for a long time.

Q posted on November 11 of 2017 this puzzling entry:

> Eye of Providence.
> Follow the bloodlines.
> What is the keystone?
> Does Satan exist?
> Does the 'thought' of Satan exist?
> Who worships Satan?
> What is a cult?
> Epstein island.
> What is a temple?
> What occurs in a temple?
> Worship?
> Why is the temple on top of a mountain?
> How many levels might exist below?
> What is the significance of the colors, design and symbol above the dome?
> Why is this relevant?
> Who are the puppet masters?
> Have the puppet masters traveled to this island?
> When? How often? Why?
> "Vladimir Putin: The New World Order Worships Satan"
> Q

It talked about the three puppet masters that Q often talks about on his posts: the Rothschild family, George Soros, and House of Saud. These three combined have unimaginable financial resources that they use in order to achieve global domination. Q claimed that the three worship Satan and the most powerful of these Satan worshippers are the Rothschilds.

According to QAnon followers, their research gleaned that the head of the family, Guy de Rothschild was declared as the Pindar. This means he is known as the CEO of

Earth as early as 1992. Before his death, Guy arranged for his position to be passed on to David Rene de Rothschild, his son. This occurred in 2003, four years before the death of Guy. In 2018, David announced that he would be passing on the leadership of the Rothschild companies to his son Alexandre. This means Alexandre is now being groomed to take over their position. This may be the what Q was referring to when he posted "follow the bloodline".

QAnon also mentioned a temple on an island named Epstein. The island is said to have underground levels where Satan worshipping rituals are regularly conducted. Bill Clinton used to visit this island frequently. According to flight logs, the former president visited this controversial island a total of 26 times. Q claimed that there are several witnesses who can describe the actual Satanic ceremonies performed at the Epstein's island. One such witness is John DeCamp.

In his book published in 1992, The Franklin Coverup: Child Abuse, Satanism and Murder in Nebrask, DeCamp was able to talk to the children who survived the said rituals done to them. He said that the children were used not just as sexual objects by certain businessmen and politicians, they were also used as drug couriers,

DeCamp also mentioned another location known as Bohemian Grove. There, a certain Larry King, not the host of a popular television show, and other personalities would bring children and have them perform sexual acts on each other. They were also made to watch other children being murdered before they are forced to eat the parts cut from the bodies. The remains were then disposed of by individuals wearing hoods. [29]

THE CHILD SEX RING ISSUE

In 2018, a woman began posting her child's reconstructed memories on Twitter. This went on for months. The memories had something to do with how Tom Hanks allegedly abused her child while she was under some form of mind control. The child was Sarah Ruth Ashcraft. The child's accounts were very specific and very disturbing.

She told her readers that she was sold by her father to be a sex doll. When questioned as to the incompleteness of her accounts, the victim claimed that it was because of the trauma that she could not recall any important details. Although the accusations were unverified, the victim's story was absorbed by the members of the QAnon movement.

It was said that Hanks was the perfect target for the Q believing crowd as he is an influential actor who donates money to the Democratic party, he is a long-time married individual, and has a generally wholesome persona. But was he a target or was his cover blown?

The problem with the issue of child abuse is that it has long been used as a propaganda tool against powerful enemies. It has been used since the medieval times on Catholics and it is still being used on politicians in the Soviet Union. It is an effective tool for otherizing the opposition and for sabotaging any sympathy than anyone might feel towards the target. Any crime involving a child, once leveled on a person, whether true or not, is difficult to shake off. This is because humans are designed to protect their offspring. Thus, once a person as said to have hurt a child, he or she is seen as a defiler of something pure. He or she is a threat to the future. And that was what was done to Hanks.

Sarah Ruth Ashcraft also leveled the same type of accusations on her own father, Hillary Clinton, her own Uncle Danny, and several other individuals. However, the victim did not provide any evidence to support these claims.

The only proof that she had for her accusation against Hanks was that her account is still active. She said that if her statement were false, Twitter would have taken down her posts. She also claimed that Tom Hanks or Hillary Clinton could easily sue for if she were lying. They were not because they know that what she posted was true.

On the same month, Dr. Dannielle Blumenthal posted support for Ashcraft. Blumenthal is a Communications Director in the National Network for Manufacturing Innovation. Her office reports directly to the National

Institute of Standards and Technology and to the White House.

Blumenthal mentioned that the reason why Ashcraft's airing of the abuses she survived is something to be believed is that there is "great danger" in going against a ring of sex traffickers. There is no glamour in it. She does not stand to gain any profit. So why would she even begin to do this if not for wanting to simply expose the truth?
To date, no formal investigation has been enforced to prove the veracity of the statements against Hanks. [29]

RED OCTOBER

In February of 2018, QAnon posted some information that seems to corroborate claims that a false flag missile has been launched against Hawaii in the previous month. It also stated that CIA-linked submarines were being hunted down by military forces. This was said to be part of Deep State's retribution for the passing of an executive order freezing the assets of any entity discovered to be involved in abuses related to human rights as well as corruption.

Various whistleblowers have alerted the public regarding the missile threat. Missile alerts were also sent to the people in the area. It was Q who declared that the missile alerts were not false alarms but a series of false flag attacks initiated by the Deep State.

Q went silent about that topic for a little while after. One month after, he posted a long entry explaining why these attacks were designed to incite war.
Q was asking his followers to analyze who would be motivated to start a war and what would they be benefiting

if it did happen. Q's bakers claim that it was obvious who was behind these attacks – Deep State. The members of this group are the ones who stand to lose so much should their assets be frozen. But, if there was a war, all these will be forgotten because the government will be too busy defending the country to go after these human rights abusers.

The bakers added that the attacks will most likely be blamed on X - North Korea. From history, we know that the surprise attack on Hawaii, Pearl Harbor specifically, was the catalyst for World War 2. If there was indeed another successful attack on the area, there will be no choice but to declare war against the alleged perpetrator.

How are false attacks being conducted? According to supporters of QAnon, there are claims that the CIA has a clandestine division that has created a Dark Fleet. This refers to missile-carrying submarines, aircraft carriers, and aircraft that work for the other side.

Q even references an old movie, "The Hunt for Red October." In the movie, the authorities were hunting down a rogue submarine. Q was allegedly telling his followers that there is a CIA submarine that has gone rogue and is now being hunted down. This submarine is seeking to launch attacks in order to precipitate a war. [30]

THE COVER-UP OF THE DEATH OF JUSTICE RUTH BADER

Seasoned reporter and editor of The Washington Post, Robert Barnes, has been writing the news for 30 years, 12 of which, he has devoted to covering the US Supreme Court.

In February 6, he claims that he has experienced a rare first in his career. He wrote article which was printed on The Post. It claimed that Justice Ruth Bader Ginsburg attended a performance in a museum in Washington.

This concert was about her life and was sponsored by her daughter-in-law. Barnes claimed that he saw the judge with his own two eyes.

Hours after his report, the rare first that he was talking about took place. People started commenting on his article and began invading his various social media accounts with messages that he was mistaken. The people were telling him that the first public appearance of Ginsburg after her surgery for cancer in December was a falsehood. It did not happen.

According to QAnon, Ginsburg has died. His followers then bombarded with Barnes for proof that what he reported was true. Unfortunately, the organizers of the event forbade all of the guests to take photos, otherwise, it would have been so easy for Barnes to prove what he saw.

As it is, doubt-mongers sent Barnes questions which, they claim, if he would not answer correctly, will prove that he lied. The questions included things like Ginsburg's appearance, the size and gender of her security detail, and more.

The rumor about Ginsburg's death may have been fanned by her failure to attend the State of the Union the night of Tuesday. While Justices Samuel Alito Jr., Stephen G. Breyer, Sonia Sotomayor, and Clarence Thomas also failed to come to the assembly, it was Ginsburg's absence that made a huge impact.

This all started when Ginsburg first missed her court's case back in January 7. She was still recovering from her December 21st surgery.

The rumor of her death appeared on the message board where Q posts his missives. The poster wondered about the real diagnosis for the judge. It also mentioned that Ginsburg may be using off-market drugs to stay alive.

One commenter claimed that the people in Washington were beginning to panic over her demise. In a few days, thousands of people were talking about Ginsburg and her death. In fact, it became one of the top searches on YouTube. The online petition for her impeachment, however, did not reach the signature goal of 5,000.

Even prominent right-wing personalities like Ben Garrison served to fan the rumor flames by wondering whether the liberals were keeping the death of Ginsburg a secret so that Trump cannot replace her with a conservative.

The musings about her death even reached mainstream media. Fox & Friends, a show on Fox News, aired a graphic about the death of Ginsburg. It was only flashed briefly and the network immediately apologized for the mistake.

This was followed by the promotion of the hashtag #WheresRuth by pro-Trump actor James Wood. The hashtag started trending on Twitter on the 28th of January. A couple of days later, Sebastian Gorka, Trump's former adviser, compounded the issue by tweeting "Still no sign" to his followers.

This is not the first rumor that targeted The US Supreme Court. In 2016, the death of Justice Antonin Scalia was also looked into by supposed rumormongers. The nature of his death was questioned, some arriving at the conclusion that it was a political hit. While there is no shred of proof to support this notion, the rumor still lives on today.

Besides the possibility that the Democrats are blocking Trump from appointing a new Supreme Court Justice, QAnon is targeting Ginsburg because it is believed that she is either a member of Deep State or a supporter of the group.

In April of 2018, Q posted several memes of Ginsburg with text that she is pushing for the lowering of the age of consent. The movement viewed this as a form of pedophile lobbying.

THE EXECUTION OF JOHN MCCAIN

It is not a secret that Donald Trump had no love for John McCain. This was on full display on the death of the Senator. While his staff urged him to acknowledge the decades of exemplary public service done by McCain, Trump chose to ignore that, sent out a generic tweet about the death, and decided to play golf instead. The flag at The White House was only briefly lowered at half-staff and during his press conference a few days later, the president obviously ignored any McCain related questions asked by the reporters. While there was no openly showed animosity, everybody knew that Trump did not want McCain around. However, was this enough to have the former Republican senator executed?

According to QAnon followers, McCain was given the codename "songbird" for being a secret agent for North Vietnam. The followers also believed that he secretly threw the elections in 2008 in favor of Obama. They circulated photos of the senator and stated that he had covert meetings with ISIS leaders. Finally, it was believed that it was he who started the "witch hunt" against President Trump which instigated the Mueller investigations. McCain was associated with the evil Clinton Foundation for a long time. In short, McCain was obviously part of Deep State. In fact, according to Alex Jones labeled McCain as the leader of the Deep State.

Rumors started circulating that the brain cancer, which was officially said to have claimed the life of the senator, was just a cover up for McCain's execution. This was allegedly "proven" during the memorial service held for him. After the ceremonies, John Kasich, a governor from Ohio, appeared on CNN and talked about McCain. He accidentally said it had only been twenty-four hours since the senator has been put to death. The keen investigative sense of many members of QAnon picked up on this slip and quickly spread the news that McCain, which Q gave a code name of No Name, has indeed been executed. They also said that execution is the penalty for committing treason.

Another popular rumor circulating among the members of the QAnon movement is that McCain may have committed suicide. Upon his death, tweets from known QAnon followers claimed that he did not succumb to cancer, rather, he took his own life in order to avoid being arrested.

This was in connection with the draining of the swamp plan that Q claims Trump is about to put into action. Before his death, QAnon followers have shared pictures of him wearing a medical boot in order to hide his ankle bracelet. They stated that the noose was tightening around the necks of the members of Deep State and in order to escape more horrendous consequences, McCain simply chose the easier way out.

These were just a few of the theories offered by the bakers of QAnon as spurred on by Q's posts. The difficulty is in finding the actual meaning of what he is trying to convey to his audience. Sometimes, the entries are so vague that his followers come up with varying, and sometimes clashing, interpretations of the message. This is then circulated among the rest of the QAnon members.

CHAPTER 3- LOOKING INTO Q

There have been probably hundreds of thousands of speculators trying to pin down the identity of the poster Q. His real name and his actual motives are just two of the many questions in people's minds when the discussion turns to the QAnon phenomenon.

Theories About Q's Identity

Some theories claim that Q is an intelligence officer from the military. Others believe that it is Donald Trump himself that is posting those cryptic messages on the message boards. Yet others posit that the QAnon movement is just part of a modern game known as an alternate reality.

With the poster's account name "Q Clearance Patriot", people, including some researchers, are certain that Q is indeed somebody who works for the government. He is either a member of the military, one of the president's advisers, or a top official from the Department of Energy. This has been rejected by other researchers as there is hardly any evidence to support this. Yes, there was that picture from the window of Air Force One, but it could just have been taken from any other aircraft. Additionally, the path taken by the flight of the presidential plane is not top secret. You can easily access it using the account @CivMilAir on Twitter.

As for the language overlap between Q and Trump, it was noted that the phrases Q use are just phrases that the president normally uses in his speeches. If a person normally says "usually" in conversation and you predicted that the person will use "usually" in the next outing, would that automatically make you an insider?

As for the Q Clearance, it has already been established that this term has no connection to any White House security clearance. The system claims that none of Q's posts required high-level security access. Nor does it evidence that he is close to or is the president.

Another theory is that Q is not a single entity but a group of people in Trump's circle. This alternate concept is backed up by the writer of the book, The Great Awakening. In his work, Peter Myer claimed that ten individuals banded together because they were worried about the future of America.

In their effort to battle the Deep State, which they are highly acquainted with, they formed an alliance and handpicked the nation's next president. They were the Q-top. The members of Q-top are so secretive and so powerful that they were able to convince Donald Trump to run for the presidency and win without him ever knowing them.

This Q-top deemed that the time to reach out to the public, what they consider as "We the People", so they assigned a member of the inner circle at the White House to covertly communicate with the masses. He was known as "QAnon" or "Q Anonymous". While pretty compelling, the author provided no tangible evidence to support this story.

Yet another theory claims that Q is the president himself. The story was already circulating but QAnon members believed this idea when they saw a picture of Trump during the gathering for the parents, students, and teachers for the Majory Stoneman Douglas High School shooting.

Right before the meeting, Trump was photographed holding his speech notes. It was facing outwards so photographers were able to zoom in and see what was on it. It contained the five topics that he will be covering during his talk. Coincidentally, just a few hours prior to that, Q posted a coded message talking about "five" security tests.

A day after that, Q posted again, this time using the picture the photographers took of Trump. He pointed out the position of the president's hand, seemingly directing the attention to the fifth point on his note card. It says, "I hear you". Q claimed that it was Trump's way of recognizing the approximately 20 million followers of QAnon and reassuring them that he does hear them.

The QAnon followers quickly stated that a veteran public speaker like Trump would never hold his note cards facing outwards accidentally. They say that his actions were deliberate to send a coded message to his followers.

Detractors, on the other hand, claim that it is impossible for President Trump to be Q. One reason is that Trump is notoriously technophobic. It is documented that Trump dislikes using the computer and often replies to electronic missives by handwriting his notes. This is then scanned and sent as a reply by his staff. Although he has been known to use Twitter, it is said that he only posts using his phone.

There is no computer to be seen in the Oval Office. Additionally, researchers compared Q's writing style with that of the president and they are not even close at all. Trump's tweeting style has numerous misspelling and typos. Q's entries, on the other hand, are error-free.

Of course, that could also be a tactic employed by the president of the United States to misdirect anybody looking into his connection with Q. A spy would often change his handwriting in order to fool the people who are trying to pin him down. The president could be deliberately tweeting erroneously in order to confuse the readers and distance himself from the persona of Q as much as possible.

Yet another theory of who Q is have emerged in late 2018. Many claim that Q is Thomas Drake. Drake is an NSA executive and decorated veteran. He turned whistleblower when his complaints regarding illegal activities and mismanagement at the NSA were ignored by his superiors.

He sent encrypted emails to certain members of the press in order to avoid discovery, but the information leak was still discovered. He is now indicted with five counts of violation of the Espionage Act. He was also charged for making false statements while he was being investigated by the FBI. [31]

Drake is an example of when a worker in sensitive agencies are forced to leak information to members of the news media in order to get the justice that they are seeking. There has been a debate as to whether he is a criminal for endangering national security or a patriot for exposing abuses in the government.

While former president Obama claimed that the act of whistleblowing by employees of the government is an act of patriotism and bravery, the indictment of Thomas Drake says otherwise. This is why many individuals believe that Drake could be Q. He already has a track record of going against the government at his own expense just to be able to expose the wrongdoings that are happening in the system. However, Drake has denied that he is Q on his Twitter account.

Besides Drake, there are a host of government employees that are currently charged with publishing intelligence on the Internet or leaking classified documents to the press. There's Stephen Jin-Woo Kim who shared information with Fox News claiming that the FBI has knowledge that North Korea will conduct a nuclear weapons test as a response to the sanctions laid on by the United Nations.

There is also Jeffrey Sterling who is a former CIA and is also charged for sharing information regarding the CIA's project Merlin. There is no dearth of government employees that would be willing to take on the mantle of anonymity if it means exposing the government's illegal activity to the masses.

Skeptics, on the other hand, do not believe that Q is an avenging patriot from the government's employ. They highly believe that QAnon is a LARP or a Live Action Roleplaying Game. Some use the term "alternative reality game". Skeptics posit that the postings and the subsequent analysis of Q's entries are done as a game and all the followers are just players. Very much like Dungeons and Dragons but is done with real people as characters.

Skeptics think that the QAnon movement was meant to be a make-believe game where an entity Q plays the part of the government mole. The Believers are supposed to play the part of the researchers who help uncover and dismantle the deep state. It merely spun out of control. It went beyond the confines of the game and even non-participants were sucked into the make-believe story without knowing it.

A Redditor pushed the LARP notion in his very widely viewed post. He offers that Q is being run by the same team that started the popular 2016 alternate reality game called BadSelfEater.

For some weeks. Strange looking dollar bills kept being found in different places all over the country. This was accompanied by a website, BadSelfEater.com, which featured a timer counting down. The dollar bills spoke ill of the US federal government and talked about some beast. This was accompanied by a Facebook page named Mr. Teeth. In it, the author left some mysterious clues.

When the timer on the website reached zero, everybody was waiting for a huge revelation. They assumed that it has something to do with the government. Some thought there was going to be a data dump on the site. Others thought that it was a marketing ploy for a movie. But, when the timer hit zero, nothing happened. Well, nothing significant. It only played a YouTube video entitled "The Great Conspiracy". The video was essentially anti-abortion propaganda. The author, T. Russel Hunter, claimed that while people were looking for clues of conspiracy and great evil, an actual evil was taking place – abortion.

While many were disappointed that nothing diabolical or life-changing was presented, a lot of people praised Hunter for his creative way of catching the public's attention in order to get his message across. [32]

Maybe this is what's happening with the QAnon movement. Could this be another elaborate strategy to get people to listen? Well, it is working. The people are listening and closely waiting for what Q will say next.

Cicada 3301 has also often been linked with QAnon because they are known for holding very complex alternate reality games, complete with codes and mysteries. Cicada 3301 is a well-known puzzle group that operated online. Manuel Chavez, a member of Cicada 3301 and goes by the handle "Defango" reportedly went online and claimed that he is behind the QAnon posts. He said that he worked with a certain math professor named William Monty McGovern in order to come up with the Q concept.

He did it by posting a YouTube video. Later on, Chavez went back on his admittance and said that it was Jerome

Corsi who is in fact Q. Jerome Corsi is a conservative pundit and known conspiracy theorist, according to people from the former administration. For twenty years, Corsi has been weaving pro-right-wing commentaries.

Everything from Obama's real birth certificate to John Kerry's military service has been dissected and analyzed by Corsi. Now, he has a direct line to Trump as he was said to have corresponded with Trump's adviser, Roger Stone. He is said to have passed on advance information regarding the release of damning Clinton emails on WikiLeaks. Because of the inside knowledge that he is showing, people started pointing to him as the person posting as Q.

Corsi himself has been talking, initially to agree regarding Q being a high-level figure in the military intelligence group. He even claimed that Q was able to prevent a coup from taking place by recruiting Donald Trump to run. A month after, Corsi commented that Q's post of a picture of a Montblanc pen is nothing more than a psychological operation of either the NSA or the CIA. This comment was backed up by Alex Jones.

Alex Jones is a host on a radio show where he talks about far-right views on certain issues. He claimed that the original QAnon account is no longer being run by an unknown official from the Trump administration. Jones said that he was able to speak to the individuals behind QAnon and has been told that the account has already been taken over.

He further claims that there are five to six people who were posting as QAnon but they no longer have control over that account. This goes with Corsi's claim that officials from the CIA and the NSA are now using the account in order to spread misinformation in an attempt to abolish the movement. [33]

In yet another theory, Jack Posobiec, a correspondent from an American network claimed that the movement was birthed by two Twitter trolls. The account was eventually taken over by a brand-new group which brought it to the 8Chan message board. The entire thing was an elaborate hoax in order to scam money from QAnon believers. Again, this sounds like something that is too absurd to happen in real life but scams do happen on a daily basis.

Similar to the notion above, some non-believers said that the movement was instigated by a 4Chan troll rather than ones on Twitter. It is not the first time that a person from 4Chan has started a disturbance for posting something untrue. The 4Chan troll made the post so believable that it fooled even the mainstream media. In 2008, a poster on 4Chan spread the gossip that Steve Jobs has suffered a heart attack.

Someone at iReport.com picked this up, maybe the 4Chan poster himself, and it spread like wildfire. iReport is a user-generated news website where literally anybody with an email can post and claim it as news. Apparently, iReport was not the only website that received this unsupported report. It was discovered later on that the owner of MacRumors.com also received the same report. It was sent via an anonymous IP address.

The story sent Wall Street into a minor panic and caused Apple's stocks to drop about 10 percent. After the story was corrected by Apple, their stocks went back up. The

Securities and Exchange Commission of the United States actually looked into this prank to identify whether it was done as intentional stock manipulation. [34]

The fact that the QAnon movement was born in 4Chan is said to be strong evidence for this 4Chan troll idea. Some say the movement is like the Steve Jobs prank that got out of control.

Maybe QAnon was a scam gone wild? Or is this theory another cover-up to confuse people and veer them away from the real identity of Q?

While researchers are busy trying to unmask Q, more are looking into how the QAnon movement exploded into the mainstream. How was he able to go from obscurity to Internet phenomenon in such a short time? Some people are claiming that he got some help.

Q MIGHT BE A HOAX BUT THE HYPE IS REAL

According to a report by NBC News, two board moderators from 4chan were instrumental in making QAnon go mainstream. Going by the usernames BarchtheScribe and Pamphlet Anon, these two reached out to Tracy Diaz, a former minor talk show host, and YouTuber, for help in making QAnon's posts go viral.

Diaz was already analyzing reports regarding the Pizzagate theory and other WikiLeaks releases. Handling another perceived conspiracy theory was not new to her. She decided to push this forward so that she can also increase her audience base. So, in November of 2017, less than a week after Q's first post on 4chan, Diaz posted a video introducing this new player. This video went on to be viewed 250,000 times. This prompted Diaz to make more Q-related posts. The channel gained over 90,000 subscribers and her QAnon videos were viewed more than 8 million times. Her Twitter account also started to soar, with nearly 100,000 new followers.

It was Diaz who recommended that they start posting on Reddit rather than let Q's posts stay in 4chan. This is so they can reach what was considered a more mainstream type of audience. She and her two 4chan moderator contacts were the ones who created the CBTS_Stream community on Reddit. As we know, this is where many of the believers lurked to talk about everything Q related. This was key in the eventual spread of the QAnon movement.

Afterward, the posts were shared on Facebook, spreading to that platform as well. Here they were able to tap older audience members. These newcomers to the movement eventually went back to 8chan to be able to see the actual posts of Q. This was at the time that QAnon migrated to the more lenient 8chan. There were some reports that the 4chan board where he originally posted on was infiltrated by the enemy. Things grew bigger that Diaz, Pamphlet Anon, and BaruchtheScribe had to hire more moderators for their Reddit board and 8chan account.

Around December of the same year, Dr. Jerome Corsi started taking an interest in what Q had to say. He began decoding the messages of Q on the Reddit boards. He also featured this on his news site – Infowars. The two 4chan moderators even made an appearance on the site. Corsi eventually disavowed the theory, claiming that there has been a takeover in the Q channel back in April of 2018.

Everything grounds to a halt when Reddit decided to shut down their board. Diaz and the two moderators were also banned from the website. At this time, Pamphlet Anon, who was identified by NBC as Coleman Rogers, decided to launch the Patriots' Soapbox. This was a YouTube Channel that broadcasted round-the-clock analysis of Q's drops. It is basically a live stream of the

Discord chatroom that is being moderated by Rogers. This also features commentary from other moderators and volunteers. [35]

Some skeptics have pointed out that Rogers may actually be Q. This rumor was further fanned by some eagle-eyed observers who noticed that during one stream on the Patriots' Soapbox, Rogers apparently logged into Q's 8chan account. This particular feed immediately cut off. During another video, Rogers was analyzing a particular Q drop when it was pointed out by his co-host that the post that they were discussing isn't on Q's feed. It was in fact posted anonymously. Majority of the audience did not put too much attention on this. As they claimed, they do not really care who Q is, as long as he keeps on talking about the truth, they will continue to listen.

Thus, this was the beginning of the rise of the QAnon movement. It was further pushed out of the fringes by so many personalities.

Q WAS NOT ALONE

Before QAnon, there were actually a number of anonymous posters or anons, that claimed that they had special access with the government. Back in 2016, a 4chan poster identified as FBIAnon started giving out information about a certain investigation that was being conducted on the Clinton Foundation. He claimed to be a high-level strategist and analyst. He shared some aspects of the battle plans of certain politicians that were planning to take out Satanists and pedophiles that were running America. Readers claim that FBIAnon was very much pro-Trump even though he claimed that everyone in the government is dirty, even Trump.

What he does is he answers questions from other people on the imageboard. For example, when he was asked if Hillary Clinton was going to be indicted, he answered that they have enough proof to take down Clinton. In fact, he claimed that they have enough to put the entire government down. He stated that got the server from Benghazi and from that server, information regarding the Clinton Foundation, which he likened to a spiderweb, was found. FBIAnon pointed out that the information found on Clinton's server could start declarations of war from other countries.

He also offered the information that Russia might leak the information that they found on the said servers because Clinton is bent on taking down the country and they have no desire to go head to head with the US. But rather than focusing on the emails, he encouraged the readers to pay attention to the Clinton Foundation instead.

One prediction of FBIAnon that did not come true was that Bill Clinton would die that year. What did come true though is his prediction that Trump would win. He claims that if it were Clinton who had won the election in 2016, America would probably go to war with Russia and China. [36]

After FBIAnon, another poster came out. His name was HLIAnon, a name that is a shortened version of High-Level Insider. This entity posted about conspiracies in riddle-form. One of the posts that he made claimed that Princess Diana was killed because she got information about the 9/11 attack and tried to stop it from happening. Another 9/11-related post claims that Hillary Clinton's campaign logo was symbolic of her secret pride about the attack, alluding that she had something to do with the horrific incident.

Just like FBIAnon, HLIAnon also answered questions posted by other users of 4chan. One of the questions posted was whether Obama genuinely won over Clinton or was it the result of genuine grassroots movement. HLIAnon answered that Obama's victory was pre-planned for a long time. When asked whether Soros was initiating the One World Government movement, he claimed that George Soros was only a puppeteer, not a puppet master. These masters, he claimed, are the members of the Bush Family. He also mentions that Obama is involved in drug trafficking. [37]

Afterward, another anon poster came to be. He started posting on the boards in the early days of 2017. He was closely followed by somebody that called himself WH Insider Anon. His first post notified the readers that something huge was about to go down and that it will probably come out on social media first before being covered by MSM like CNN. He also talked about the Uranium scandal and revealed some key players. Finally, he posted about the DNC and what they might do regarding the email leaks.

They brought attention to these notions before QAnon started posting. They began attracting followers and prepared the audience for Q. After he started posting, he gathered more followers and started the movement. Then, more personalities threw their hats into the ring to keep the movement alive.

It was these people that paved the way for Q to reach more audience. Are they connected to each other? Nobody knows this for sure. But their message is clear. People cannot just trust anybody blindly.

THE OTHER PEOPLE THAT FANNED THE QANON FLAMES

While mainstream media vilified the QAnon movement as a complex hoax, a lot of so-called conservative pundits have become supporters of this phenomenon. These new voices have given the movement new life.

One of the well-known personalities pushing the QAnon movement forward is the former pitcher of the Boston Red Sox, Curt Schilling. This athlete turned political commentator has started sharing QAnon videos on his account on Facebook. His first post was a video created by an anon that claims that all the US presidents starting from Ronald Reagan were "criminal" that is allied to an international cabal responsible for nearly all the evils on earth.

The narrator of the video goes on to blame this group for orchestrating the shooting in Las Vegas and in Sandy Hook. He also claimed that they were responsible for hijacking North Korea and forcing the leader of that country to start producing nuclear weapons. The cabal was said to have enough clout that they forced Miley Cyrus to give up her family-friendly image in order to destabilize the structure of the American Family. As a solution, the narrator tells the believers of QAnon, was to form an alliance between Trump, Russia's Vladimir Putin, and the military in order to ultimately stop Deep State. [38]

Another staunch supporter of the movement is the owner of Big-League Politics. This right-wing blog featured an article on the "anons". These are the entities that attempt to decode the clues and riddles that QAnon posts. The site called the anons a group of "revolutionary citizens" who put a lot of time and effort in order to explain Q's missives in layman terms so that more people can understand what is truly happening in Trump's battle with the Deep State. The article from BLP also talks about the alleged attempt to assassinate Trump, when a missile was fired at Air Force One from an unknown location near Singapore.

Another blogger and known theorist, Michael Moates, showed his support for QAnon by telling his readers to keep a close eye on Q. He claims that because of a non-disclosure agreement, he cannot reveal any relevant information and that all he can say was for people to pay attention to what QAnon was posting. While this seems vague, he was able to direct a lot of his followers to start reading more about what QAnon has been talking about.

Yet another celebrity supporter of Q has been making waves on Twitter. Roseanne Barr, a famous American comedian who is making a comeback on television, also promoted QAnon. On the 31th of March, back in 2018, after promoting her revived sitcom, Barr started tweeting praises about President Trump. She was specifically talking about how Trump has successfully broken up child trafficking rings that were in high places.

She followed this tweet with retweets of articles detailing the information about untold stories of what the Trump government is doing in order to destroy these pedophile rings. One such link led to a website that claimed that the police was able to arrest 1500 criminals by the second month of Donald Trump's presidency. These criminals were all connected to pedophile rings that involved politicians and Hollywood stars as well.

While Barr did not write anything about QAnon on her tweets, the things that she retweeted were definitely theories that were being pushed by Q. Additionally, Barr made a public request for Q to contact her through her DM.

On March 23, the comedian retweeted a summary of the theories that were posted by Q, particularly on how the newly passed omnibus spending bill was going to affect how law enforcement would go after pedophile rings.

Unfortunately, mainstream media researchers have discredited the child trafficking statistics that Barr was sharing. The data that was used for the given regarding the sex trafficking busts during Trump's time was said to be made up. Very few of the arrests which was cited by its writer, Liz Crokin, were actually related to sex trafficking.

Of course, alleged made up numbers did not prevent Barr's fans from sharing her retweeted links.

Some might say that the pundits and celebrities who supported Q simply rode his tails to push their own agenda. Bloggers and YouTubers simply wanted more people to read and watch their material. Celebrities wanted to gain more recognition. Pundits wanted people to talk about them. Just like the entrepreneurs who manufactured Q merchandise on Amazon, these people cashed in on the movement. In these cases though, it could be considered a two-way street this time because they also served as the means for QAnon to rise out of the recesses of anonymity to global recognition. With every tweet, YouTube video, and Facebook share, these personalities reached more people and allowed them to get to know the truths that QAnon is trying to spread. These personalities were instrumental in letting Q gain more fans.

WHY PEOPLE BELIEVE Q

There are many reasons why people believe the truths that Q is giving out. Some want some validation that their decision of voting for Trump is a good one. Others want something to blame for the quality of their life, and Deep State is as good an enemy as any. Yet others, just like the anons of Q, see some truth in what QAnon has been posting, despite many of his predictions failing to come to fruition.

With what the majority, and mainstream media, see as Donald Trump's bumbling in the White House, it has gotten a little difficult for Trump's supporters to justify their decision to vote for him. They were being told by the people in their families and communities that they made a huge mistake and that the country has been plunged in chaos when they voted for an apparently incompetent candidate.

Notions like the ones pushed forward by QAnon creates some form of order out of the alleged chaos. QAnon has been promising his followers that everything, even the perceived missteps of Trump, are all part of the plan.

When the QAnon movement's main beliefs – that Robert Mueller was working with Trump in order to expose thousands of personalities who are said to be cannibalistic pedophiles – failed to come true, many believed that it would be the end of the movement. No, the Mueller report made no mention of any cannibals, child murderers, or pedophiles. Yes, it resulted in arrests, but the people were not the ones that Q promised. And yet, the QAnon movement endured. Are his believers to resistant to facts that they would rather cling to the apparent falsehoods that were being promoted by Q?

It is not just the mainstream news outlets and left-leaning groups that are dismissing the QAnon movement and the truths dropped by Q as ridiculous. Even some major supporters of Trump publicly claim that QAnon is just a scam or a hoax. So why are people still fervently waiting for the next breadcrumb to drop? Is it pride? Are people too ashamed to admit that they made a mistake when they voted for Trump? Or, is there a much bigger reason for them believing that everything is going according to plan?

Now we go to the second reason. People need to find something or someone to blame when things do not go their way. With the emergence of QAnon, there is now an explanation of why people remain poor. Why despite all the advances in medicine, droves of us still die every day. It also explains why there are rifts between countries. It is all because of Deep State, or whatever it is that you want to call the evil assemblage of people that control nearly every aspect of our lives.

They spread disinformation so that people will remain ignorant and poor. If you are too busy making a living, you wouldn't seek out to understand why no matter what you do, your situation doesn't improve. If you are too busy dying, you wouldn't look too closely at the type of medicine that your doctor is giving you. You just accept what they tell you to be factual. So, Deep State is a good villain that can be blamed for each and every misfortune. This is similar to how people view religion. When misfortune hits them, they are given an out because they either think that the misfortune was caused by the devil or that it is part of God's plan. There is a relief from accountability.

A certain political analyst that goes by the moniker Joe M explained on Twitter that people want to believe the entries of QAnon because it is bringing the people together. Battling the Deep State gives people a common enemy. And rallying behind the man who has been chosen to take down Deep State has given people a common purpose. This is the power of QAnon. He was able to attract the attention of the people who are "awake" enough to want to be a part of the movement. And, failed predictions aside, the movement is very much alive.

Yet another reason given out by analysts in their attempt to explain the undying appeal of QAnon is its game-like quality. Even people who are not interested in politics get caught up in the excitement of waiting for a clue left by the game-maker, Q. As soon as the drop is made, all the believers rush to solve the riddle and try to match it with what's happening in the real world. This could be why there are now dozens of so-called QAnon experts who post their analysis on Twitter or YouTube. Some even started their own pages just to be able to freely express their ideas.

Yet, most of the people who fervently follow Q and excitedly await his next clue truly believe and see some truth in what he is saying. They understand that in order to truly drain the so-called swamp, the government that is entrenched by traitors and evil doers, there must be some subterfuge involved. Failed predictions do not faze them because they know that these are necessary so that Q doesn't give up Trump's strategy. Of course, this must be done because he can never be sure who gets to read his drops. They must be true enough to make sense to his bakers but not too simple that their enemies get the real picture too.

HOW THE Q PHENOMENON HAS AFFECTED THE REAL WORLD

While many alleged conspiracy theories that started out in the shadowy depths of message boards live and die an unmourned death, there are some that manage to get out and enter popular social networks. The entrance of the QAnon movement into the mainstream websites could be a testament to how many people believe that Q is legitimately telling them the truth.

Followers have started posting their own analyses of Q's postings on their own YouTube channels. If you do a quick search on the platform, you would be presented with hundreds of videos talking about the clues that QAnon left. Some avid followers have also taken to posting accusatory comments on trailers of movies featuring personalities involved in the theory regarding the alleged child sex ring.

Among those who were targeted by followers was Tom Hanks and Steven Spielberg. While Q has not explicitly mentioned their names, the celebrities were still tagged by followers based on the clues left for them. Cemex, a Mexican company that manufactures cement, was also involved in this as a vehicle for child trafficking. This name was specifically mentioned by Q on a post.

For a time, if one conducted a search on these names, the top videos would feature videos accusing the entities of being involved in pedophilia. Prior to this, the followers of QAnon heavily shared these accusations on Reddit and Twitter. It was no surprise that it has grown very popular by the time it hit YouTube.

After YouTube was contacted by NBC News for comments regarding this movement, some videos of Q followers began dropping in ranking.

An organization decided to make real-life actions following the QAnon followers' campaign against Cemex. A group known as "Veterans on Patrol" found and staked out an encampment they claim to be Cemex's child sex trafficking camp. [39]

After their report, investigators and even a police cadaver dog was brought to the area but found no evidence to prove the claim of the group. This did not stop the group from giving up on their notion.

Even after several reassurances from the police, the group remained stolid in their conviction and stayed at the area, often live streaming their stay on Facebook and YouTube. It's leader, Michael Lewis Arthur Mayer, claimed that he accidentally found the site after suffering from a tire blowout at a nearby highway.

His group decided to look closer at the wooded area

where they subsequently found tarps attached to tree branches, pieces of clothing, some items made for children, and an old tank that was partially buried in the dirt. It was this tank that convinced Meyer and his group that this area was where children were held there. They even saw a tree that had straps attached to it. The group claimed that it was a "rape tree".

The group's initial live stream video of the encampment blew up and was viewed more than 700,000 times. Subsequent posts have been viewed over 2.5 million times. Other bloggers and YouTube personalities began featuring these videos, offering their own analysis on the connection between this piece of land and Cemex. All this despite not being able to show any solid proof of the connection between that abandoned land to Deep State.

Mayer eventually was arrested for felony trespassing. The page housing the videos posted by Veterans on Patrol were also taken down by Facebook. Many have conjectured that somebody was getting worried at the amount of publicity that the group was generating and they believed that further investigation on the area would eventually lead to solid evidence of the sex ring. This was why powerful forces made sure that the group and their evidence went away. [40]`

Again, the mere fact that police dismissed the conjecture coming from Mayer's group so easily was viewed by the followers of QAnon as show of power of the Deep State. They claimed that somebody from the inside was able to influence the rest to abandon the search despite being shown the rape tree and abandoned clothing.

One of the effects that Q has been accused of encouraging is fanning the flames of the public's distrust of the press. Most QAnon followers claim that they have stopped getting their news from mainstream media because these are almost always tainted by the Deep State.

In August of 2018, the crowd allegedly made up primarily of the supporters of QAnon, rushed the area where the members of the press were gathered and harassed them. This occurred right after one of the president's "Make America Great Again" rallies.

Video footages showed the crows surrounding the enclosure and began to jeer and swear at the assembled press. Jim Acosta, a news anchor from CNN, was the target of some of the verbal abuses said to have been hurled by the crowd.

Acosta said that this was just a sample of the hostility that results from the spread of theories that, he claimed, were totally unfounded. Even the former press secretary, Anthony Scaramucci, condemned these acts. He said that the free press was important and needs to be protected.

Sarah Huckabee Sanders, the Press Secretary of the White House has also spoken that the president denounced any entity that incites violence against another. She claims that that type of behavior is not something that the president supports. However, with the president's rhetoric that anything not going his way were fake news manufactured by the media, it is difficult to undo the growing notion that the press is the enemy of the masses. [41]

But, the question that most QAnon followers ask is, "Isn't the press the enemy?" Again, with the emergence of some proof that mainstream media does control the information it releases and sometimes writes articles in the tone that they wish to imbue on what should be neutral, isn't it normal for the people to question the motive of the press each and every time news comes out? This is why more and more people are turning to alternative sources of news.

There is now a growing mistrust against mainstream media that people automatically question the motive of the release and broadcast of any piece of news. This is what QAnon wants its followers to do. He doesn't want people to accept what they are being told simply because the information comes from a "reputable" source. Who is the reputable source?

Even online retailers have joined the bandwagon either to support the movement or, at least, earn a few bucks off the followers of the enigmatic Q.

If you do a search of the term "QAnon" on Amazon's website, you will be presented with over a thousand different merchandise options. You can get a hat, mug, pet collars, bumper stickers, or T-shirt emblazoned with a big "Q".

For a while, QAnon products were labeled with "Amazon's Choice" to show that these were premium items. It was only until it started getting criticized for serving as a marketplace for racist merchandise and for condoning white supremacy in a report conducted by NBC News did they stop putting the label on items related to the QAnon movement.

The retail giant did not suffer much from this action though. Amazon reported a $1.6 billion profit for the first three months of 2018. A huge chunk of that coming off QAnon sales. Amazon is not alone in riding the tails of the QAnon movement towards huge profits.

QDrops and app developed so that followers can easily keep track of posts made by Q was reported to be the most downloaded entertainment app of that year. It enjoyed a level of popularity that other big games, like MLB's RBI Baseball '18 and Minecraft, experiences. After an inquiry done by NBC News, Apple decided to pull the app from its iTunes store. It is still downloadable from Google's Play Store though.

One of the products that can be bought online is a QAnon patch. This product got one of the followers in trouble. On November of 2018, Vice President Mike Pence had his picture taken with his group of SWAT team members. These were the men who protected him during his stay in South Florida.

There was nothing that happened out of the ordinary and the pictures were happily posted on Twitter. This was when the commotion started. The observant public noticed that one of the officers, Deputy Mike Patten was wearing a weird patch on his tactical vest. It was a big letter Q on red fabric. Underneath were the words "Question the Narrative".

This shared photograph not only caught the attention of the public, but it also caught the attention of Q himself. He shared the picture and wrote, "It's spreading."

While the members of the QAnon movement cheered for the brazen display of support done by the officer, his employer did not. In fact, the Sheriff's Office of Boward County called in Sergeant Patten in order to reprimand him and tell him that he was effectively removed from the SWAT team. He was demoted and reassigned to a new department.

His supervisor from the sheriff's office wrote on the disciplinary report that Patten's actions of showing unity for a group that is steeped in controversy were not in alignment of the law enforcement's core value. Additionally, he was also reprimanded for wearing a patch of the SWAT insignia on his uniform.

According to reports, Sergeant Patten was not sporting the patch the entire time. It was only during the time when Vice President Pence asked to thank the team who escorted him back to the airport did the officer put on the patch. Mr. Pence has since deleted the post containing the controversial photograph.

It was widely speculated that Sergeant Patten was disciplined for being a part of a movement that was moving against Deep State, but it was explained that the wearing of a patch was strictly prohibited. It is a way of silencing the members of the group so they cannot spread the truth.

This was not the first time that Patten got in trouble for displaying the SWAT insignia. A year before, during a presentation of equipment to the sheriff's office, Patten was filmed placing a pair of night vision goggles on a helmet that has been adorned by the SWAT insignia. It is unknown whether he has been reprimanded for that infraction as well. [42]

What may be considered as the ultimate proof that QAnon has entered the realm of real-life was its inclusion in Time Magazine's list of 25 Most Influential People on the Internet in 2018. The magazine acknowledged that the movement is so massive that it has been discussed and analyzed in over 130,000 videos on YouTube.

Not to mention the countless websites that wait for each and every drop of Q's breadcrumbs in order to scrutinize the minute details in his entry. Celebrities are now also acknowledging QAnon. Actress Roseanne Barr even tweeted that she wants Q to contact her.

But, while the rise of a fringe movement can be said to be meteoric and unprecedented, it appears like forces are working in order to take down this group. It may be coincidental that platforms started imposing stricter rules for their users at the time that Q was posting his crumbs and media outlets all deciding to write negative articles about what they claim to be the biggest and craziest conspiracy theory of all, but it could also be an orchestrated attack in order to silence Q.

CHAPTER 4 – THE FALL OF Q?

From the very beginning, Q's missives were already cryptic. His clue-like messages need interpreters for a regular reader to understand. However, during the start, he did not shy away from revealing specific dates of supposed actions. It was only after his followers started expressing frustration that Trump keeps missing Q's deadlines that his posts began turning ambiguous. It was during this transition that many started questioning if his intelligence is still legitimate. Is he purposely being more cryptic because he is under threat from Deep State? Or has he been burned from the many predictions that he made that did not come true? Analysts claimed that Q cannot afford to have more predictions not coming to fruition because that will be a death blow to an already ailing, according to them, group.

The Failed Predictions or So Some Think

Mainstream media is portraying the QAnon movement as a fragmented group. One of the main reasons for this disjointedness is the failing credibility of the source – Q.

There are two main events that analysts claimed to be the final nails on the proverbial coffin.

The first one had something to with the 2018 midterm elections. Back in May, QAnon was already hinting at a "red wave". This claim was that the Republicans will win big. Q said that this will bring justice and strength to the Trump government, which he will need for an event that will happen on November 11 of that year.

Source: https://www.dailydot.com/layer8/qanon-jeff-sessions-2018-midterms/

Over the next few weeks, Q kept on bolstering the hope of his followers, making promises of the "red wave" which he likened to a tsunami that would wipe out the evil controlling group that was manipulating America.

Contrary to his predictions, the Republicans did not win big during that election. When the announcement was made that the Democrats won the House, there was an explosion of anguish from the Q followers. Some questioned if Trump really had a plan. Others started questioning whether Q really did know the truth. Q was quick to appease his followers stating that, as before, everything that is happening is in accordance with the original plan.

He also restated that despite what it looks like. Trump was still in control. He further states that they, meaning the group of Trump, got what they wanted. Again, the followers go back to the hope that the release of the sealed indictments that Trump was allegedly unleashing on the Democrats will allow the Republicans to take back the House of Representatives. This seemed to appease some of the followers.

The next event that is seen as another reason for the weakening of the follower's faith in Q is what Trump decided to fire Attorney General Jeff Sessions. Until that time, Sessions was a huge favorite of the Q followers. Q has been building him up as an ally who was the mastermind behind the plan of the mass arrests of Clinton, Obama, and other evil doers.

But right around the beginning of November in 2018, rumors started to fly that Trump was about to rid himself of his former close political ally. Trump never forgave Sessions for recusing himself from the probe done regarding Trump's ties with Russia and their hand in the 2016 election. During an afternoon presscon, reporters asked Trump regarding the job security of his then Deputy Attorney General and Attorney General. Trump evaded the questions, simply stating that he is looking at different things. Three hours after, Trump announced that he was replacing Sessions with Matthew Whitaker using his Twitter account. It was later discovered that Sessions resigned at the request of Trump.

The firing of another supposed player in Trump's secret plans sent many followers into a tailspin. So much for their hopes that the mass arrest would allow the Republicans to take back what was supposed to be theirs.

According to a popular debunker of conspiracy theories, Mike Rothschild, these events occurring back to back was simply too much for those whose faith in QAnon was already shaky. The rest has retreated to Voat, the social network where the community moved to upon their banning from Reddit. Some expressing frustration and impatience for Trump's actions. More strived to remind each other that there is a plan and that they just have to have faith. There, they patiently awaited the next drop that Q will give.

What could be troubling for many is the suggestion that the QAnon followers begin forming citizen militias and begin taking concrete steps in eliminating the Deep State. [43]

QAnon debunking videos have also started cropping up. This is doing a lot of damage to the ranks of the followers. With their faith already wavering, watching these videos can ultimately convince them that they have been duped.

This is exactly what QAnon has been talking about. Followers have already opened their eyes to being more open about the truth. By allowing themselves to be influenced by the "truths" that others have chosen for them, they are undoing the great awakening that they have gone through.

QAnon maintains that Trump is still following the path that was assigned to him. Whatever failures that people think he is experiencing are all part of the long-term plan. Some of the failures are misdirection to keep his enemies guessing. It is important that people keep the trust and the truth will be revealed in the end.

Are these failed predictions enough to kill the faith of QAnon followers? Probably for some. However, history has taught us that there are instances when QAnon says one thing and then what happens is another. One great example was in Alice and the Wonderland incident.

According to anons, QAnon's predictions about the indictments of Clinton, Podesta, and Abedin was merely misdirection to give Deep State a false sense of control.

All the while, Trump was eyeing crippling Deep State by taking out one of its main funders – the corrupt members of the House of Saud. This, according to Q believers, was evidenced by the unreported trip of Jared Kushner to Saudi Arabia. It was reported by the anons that Kushner, husband of Ivanka Trump, with the blessing of President Trump secretly met with King Salman and his son in order to provide them with intelligence regarding the illegal activities of the country's princes and other top officials.

The result of this is the 2017 declaration of Martial Law where various important members of the House of Saud were purged. The targets were the senior princes, past and present ministers, owners of television stations, the leader of a significant military branch, and a major shareholder of many global companies such as Apple, Citibank, Twentieth Century Fox, Lyft, and Twitter. The anons claim that the White Rabbit were the corrupted princes that were providing money to the cabal of evildoers.

This purge sent fear shockwaves not only all over the kingdom but throughout the world. The loss of source of considerable funding should be a huge blow to Deep State. They were probably blindsided because they were expecting an attack in the United States. After dealing with the Wonderland and the White Rabbit, QAnon claims that Trump will now turn his eye on America and then to Asia and the United Kingdom.

Unfortunately, this hasn't been followed by any concrete steps by Trump or his people. After the Saudi coup, nothing has been visibly done to further cripple Deep State. This is the reason why people are starting to get antsy. Some are getting impatient. What will be the next step? Q has been a little too quiet about that.

QANON-RELATED INCIDENTS THAT PUT THE MOVEMENT IN BAD LIGHT

Mainstream media pegs one of Trump's political rallies as the coming-out event for the QAnon movement. It was the rally in Tampa, Florida last August 1. In the Fox News broadcast, the camera kept on catching members of the crowd who were wearing "Q" shirts and holding up "We are Q" placards. CNN reporter, Jim Acosta, was even urged by an attendee to ask the president about the QAnon group. This was a time when QAnon was still just a minor entity on the Internet, known mainly by those who hang out on 4chan and other message boards.

It was on this day that the world got a first look of the growing movement. It could be said that August 1 of 2018 is also the day when the QAnon movement members showed that it can be violent. This is one of the things that skeptics are worried about – that members will be provoked to do something rash based on what Q is telling them. After the MAGA Rally, as the reporters were wrapping up their pieces, the members of the audience surrounded the fence that separated the press from the rest of the people. They started heckling the members of the media. They cursed at and screamed profanity at the reporters. One even held up a sign alluding to the death of Seth Rich. This was alluding to the claim that the Democratic National Committee had Rich killed for allegedly leaking sensitive intelligence and emails back in 2016. [44]

This show of aggression prompted people to ask the Press Secretary, Sarah Huckabee Sanders, what the President thinks of this. She claims that the president clearly denounces any group that would provoke violence against others. She added that the president doesn't offer his support to any individual or group that shows and support this type of behavior. Of course, QAnon followers view this denouncement as the president's way of getting the group out of the limelight.

Being able to see the truth and knowing the evil doings of the enemy can naturally make any individual want to take action. On June 15, another QAnon believer did take action. Matthew Wright used an armored vehicle in order to block traffic on a bridge very near Hoover Dam. For 90 minutes, Wright refused to budge from the Mike O'Callaghan-Pat Tillman Memorial Bridge. He was holding a sign that is asking for the release of the real OIG report.

He brought an AR-15 rifle, several magazines of ammunition, a handgun, and even a flash-bang device. He drove across the said bridge and went on US Highway 93 before being turned back the police roadblock that was set up there. He eventually surrendered when his armored vehicle got stuck on the dirt road as authorities flattened his tires using spike strips. Luckily, nobody got injured during the entire event.

Again, mainstream media blamed QAnon for spreading his message and inciting people to commit such brazen acts just to out the truth that he has been disseminating. They have labeled Wright as a right-wing extremist. Allegedly, Wright wanted to see the unredacted report of the Justice Department inspector general. This said report has details about Deep State, according to QAnon. Wright simply wanted to see the truth. He also expressed frustration that Trump promised to have certain personalities arrested but have yet done so. This is exactly what the press has been warning people about. When fervent Q followers fail to see any progress in the president's supposed plan, they might get frustrated and do something potentially dangerous just to get things rolling. [45]

Even while in jail, Wright kept on writing letters to Trump as well as other elected officials citing QAnon mottos – For where we go one, we go all. He was still asking for the truth. The problem is that the truths that mainstream media was releasing don't really go with the truth that QAnon was revealing to his followers. And this is causing some sort of distress to the followers. Q keeps reassuring his believers that there is a reason for all his and Trump's actions. You cannot trust yet what you see now because it is all part of an elaborate and long-playing plan to get rid of Deep State. How long will this reason keep the peace among believers?

Not even a month after the Hoover Dam incident, another alleged QAnon-related event occurred. On the 29th of July, back in 2018, QAnon posted the link to Michael Avenatti's website. He also posted photographs of the lawyer's office building in Newport Beach. The message that went with this post was "Buckle up". Q also posted a picture of an unknown man who seems to be holding a cellphone and an unidentified thin object. The photo apparently was meant to send Avenatti a message. The photo was taken near the lawyer's office building. Because of that, the Newport Beach Police Department started an investigation to see if anybody was indeed stalking the lawyer.

Why was QAnon targeting Avenatti? This was because the lawyer used to represent Stormy Daniels in a lawsuit against the president. Back in January of 201, The Wall Street Journal exposed that a little before the 2016 presidential elections, Daniels was allegedly paid by Michael Cohen, Trump's former personal lawyer, an undisclosed amount of money to sign a nondisclosure agreement regarding her alleged affair with Donald Trump back in 2006. Daniels then decided to sue Cohen and the president, claiming that the NDA was not valid.

Avenatti responded to this alleged QAnon harassment by tweeting that the more the believers of the movement attacked him, the more confident he is that the suit is a significant threat to the president. Eventually, Avenatti and Daniels part ways. However, this incident was again used by the media to show that QAnon and his followers are capable of harassing personalities should they choose to do so. One picture alone can send the police scurrying.

What could be considered as the latest Q-related incident is the cancellation of the Grass Valley Charter School fundraiser. This was supposed to take place on May 11th of 2019. It all started with the tweet of James Comey,

Former head of the FBI, in April. He used the hashtag #FiveJobsIveHAd. The five jobs' first letters were GVCSF. This was later interpreted by Q's anons as a threat to the Grass Valley Charter School.

Source: https://www.bbc.com/news/world-us-canada-48231708

The followers claimed that Comey could be planning a terror attack at the event. Other anons saw the hashtag to be an anagram of the phrase "five jihads". Additionally, the time stamp for when Comey posted his tweet was said to be related to the attack on 9-11. Anons claimed that Comey could be planning to stage what they consider to be false flag attacks. These believers passed on the information to authorities which in turn informed the school. The school, after receiving notice from the police, decided to call off the event for fear that internet vigilantes would go to the venue to stop the former FBI director should he "pursue" his attack plan. [46]

MAINSTREAM MEDIA'S TAKES A CLOSER LOOK AT QANON'S ORIGIN

Who or what is behind the QAnon posts is a hotly debated topic on and offline? People have been working hard to uncover the person, or group, that has been persistently posting entries on 4chan, and then eventually on 8chan, for over a year. Perhaps it is the members of the mainstream media that works the hardest in unmasking the real identity of this entity. After all, if they found out that Q was not really a government official, this would certainly do a lot of damage to his credibility. What would people think if QAnon was revealed to be just a blogger? Would they still believe the information that he is passing along?

One of the most persistent theories is that the people behind QAnon are just 4chan trolls. It is now common knowledge that the birthplace of QAnon, 4chan, is made up of a community of anons who are well known for their ability to hatch up pranks, some very dangerous, that are so elaborate and believable that they fool even the members of MSM or mainstream media.

4chan trolls are not new to creating hoaxes. One example is when they started and successfully spread a rumor about Steve Job succumbing to a heart attack. The rumor first appeared in iReport.com, a user-generated news website. iReport.com was a place where citizen journalists can post news that they researched and created. Anybody can post on this website as long as that person provides an email address. The website came under fire when a user used their site to post a false report that the CEO of Apple, Steve Jobs, suffered from a serious heart attack. What gave the rumor credibility was it being picked up by other blogs such as SAI or Silicon Alley Insider. SAI is a financial news blog based in New York. It is an established and trusted blog, which is why people believed the news.

Not only was this an attack on Jobs, but the fake news piece also sparked panic on Wall Street. It was enough to send Apple's stock into a dive. Its share price went down by 10% before correcting later that same day. The stock price began to plummet when the article came out on SAI despite being unconfirmed. Not even an hour after posting, SAI updated their report to say that Apple has categorically denied the story on iReport. A few minutes after, the stock price started to recover.

It was Arnold Kim, owner, and operator of the MacRumors.com blog, who did the research and found out that the same story that came out on iReport was being circulated by members of the 4chan community.

If the members of 4chan are savvy enough to create and circulate such a damaging rumor, it is not such a reach to think that they could be behind the QAnon posts. They definitely are smart enough to get their hands-on sensitive information that they could be using in order to create the Q drops.

Back in August of 2008, former governor of Alaska, Sarah Palin, had her email account hacked. The person who broke into her account was a 4chan user. David Kernell, then a college student, is the son of Mike Kernell, state representative of Memphis. The young Kernell accessed Palin's emails using the password recovery feature of Yahoo. He then proceeded to post screenshots of Palin's emails on /b/ imageboard of 4chan.

While Kernell's hacking attempt may seem simplistic, other members of the 4chan community are adept at hacking more secured accounts. That is why it is not surprising if they were the ones behind QAnon entries. This is certainly what James Hitchcock firmly believes. He is an editorial assistant from the New York Times. This theory was supported by Buzzfeed, a digital media company. They claimed that the QAnon movement is a prank that has gone overboard. They also claimed that this prank is based on an obscure novel from Italy entitles "Q".

Other people believe that QAnon was perpetuated by a handful of conspiracy theorists in order to increase their audience. It is also said that the group wanted to promote the "Make America Great Again" cause. This theory was put forward by The War Economy, a self-proclaimed Anti-Q researcher. He was backed up by UNIRock, a streamer who makes and posts videos on YouTube. UNIRock claimed that he was able to communicate with the actual Q. He also stated that there were 5 Q entities in total.

Some also say that QAnon is just a LARP. This stands for Live Action Role Play. As explained, a LARP is a make-believe game. In this case, Q plays a significant role of a government mole. The followers play the role of analysts or researchers. The goal is to overpower an entity called Deep State. There are many who believe that this was just a game meant for the people on 8chan. Unfortunately, the word got out and the game spun out of control. This theory is being promoted by Jack Posobiec.

So far, he has not been able to provide any actual proof of this notion being true. One Redditor that goes by the name QPredictedPiss claims that he knows the people who are running the QAnon LARP. He stated that they were the same ones who organized BadSelfEater. This was an alternate reality game that was started in 2016. Yet another faction stated that its Cicada 3301 that organized this game. One of the members of the group said that he worked with William Monty McGovern, a math professor, in creating QAnon. The video of this admission has already been taken down.

There are many other theories about the origin of QAnon. Some say that it is simply a Russian PsyOp in order for the country to continue meddling in the affairs of the US government. This notion is being promoted by one popular grey hat hacktivist called The Jester. He claims that we would eventually find out that QAnon is just a another GRU from Russia. It is designed to make Americans more susceptible to pushing for policies that favor the Russian government. GRU stands for Glavnoye razvedyvatel'noye upravleniye which is the foreign military intelligence agency of the Russian Federation.

Many sceptics think that QAnon is very pro-Russia. His posts has been casting doubts regarding the alleged meddling of the Russian government. He is critical of John McCain, ho in turn is very critical of Russia. And, Q aggressively pushes the notion regarding Seth Rich and his alleged murder over leaked DNC documents. This theory is also being pushed by Russian entities as it absolves them of hacking the Democratic National Committee.

One of the strongest proof that has been laid out regarding the GRU theory is when Q urged attacks on the Global Engagement Center. The GEC is an initiative from the State Department that is tasked to fight against meddling of the Russian government. Why would somebody who is supposedly a patriot promote an attack on a group that is tasked to help the US maintain its independence?

Others claim that it is a Pied Piper Operation established by the Deep State. These people believe that this group is seeking to blind people from Deep State's activities by misdirecting them.

A journalist based in New Zealand, Suzie Dawson, explained that the strategy exhibited by Q is textbook PsyOp strategy. He started with establishing his credibility and then worked to get into the minds of his followers and cultivate devotion from them using spiritual concepts. This was backed by WikiLeaks's Julian Assange. He claims that QAnon was being used by the White House in order to reduce the public's pressure on the president. Q has effectively convinced his followers to stop government persecution. If you look at it closely, this notion makes sense. Since the arrival of Q, many people have stopped questioning the actions of Trump, believing that whatever he is doing now, whether it makes sense or not, is all part of his long-term plan.

Yet others believe that the identity of QAnon can be found simply by looking at the people are always around Trump.

One of those people is Dan Scavino. They believe that Trump's Social Media director could be posting all the QAnon messages in order to make the president appear better than he actually is. According to reports, Scavino is often in charge of writing Trump's tweets for him. Him being Q explains why the president's tweets and the entries of Q sometimes have the same wording. One example is when Trump posted a tweet lambasting the investigation against him and his campaign. The president asked in his tweet why Mueller and 13 Angry Democrats weren't looking into the lies that emanated from the FBI and the DOJ. The number was later on changed to 17. This was said to have been done so that the communication would line up with QAnon related concepts. Remember that the 17th letter of the alphabet is Q.

In another Tweet, Trump talked about the Congressional races by posting "5 for 5!" QAnon is known to post the same number 5:5 on 4chan.

While mainstream media is trying its best to find out who is the person responsible for this phenomenon, many believers of Q maintain that they do not care who is the person who is doing the typing. What matters is the message. However, it is not known how followers will actually react should they find out that Q is not really a White House insider.

ACCESS DENIED FOR Q AND HIS FOLLOWERS

A year after the very first breadcrumb was dropped by QAnon, it has clawed its way out of 4Chan insignificance into the light of mainstream media. People who are talking about each clue presented by Q are not just the lurkers who stay within the confines of the murky message boards, or people who are classified by media as alt-right theorists. In Florida, polls showed that a majority of the citizens there know about QAnon enough to have an opinion about his posts. These are regular people.

So-called experts likened the QAnon movement to religious cults because of the pattern of its growth and the similarity of enticements that it uses to attract believers. They claim that because the opinions posted by QAnon were so detached from what most people are trained to see, those who have the same opinions feel isolated. With the Internet, these people were able to reach out to like-minded individuals. They get to share their views without being persecuted and mocked. Additionally, it allows them to become a part of "something big".

However, the numerous disappointments that the

QAnon believers have experienced in the past two years of Q's existence are starting to take a toll. People are starting to question whether there is real truth behind what QAnon has been posting, or have they all been duped by an online troll? It doesn't help that entities are starting to pressure various media platforms into preventing the bakers from spreading the truth.

It is undebatable that Reddit was crucial in the emergence of the QAnon movement. It enabled this phenomenon to move from the fringes of the Internet to more mainstream circles. This is why a lot of people keeping track of the QAnon progress were surprised when specific QAnon Reddit communities were banned from the website last September 12, 2018. On the subreddit page for the /r/greatawakening, the management posted that it was being banned due to recurrent violations of the content policy terms. According to one of the site's spokespersons, the policies that they violated had something to do with harassment, violence, and dissemination of other people's personal information.

Considering that the QAnon community was its largest community, with over 70,000 subscribers, it is astounding that Reddit decided to cut off the entire group. These subscribers were responsible for over 10,000 comments a day before being cut off. Even the backup subreddits that were formed were hunted down and banned as well. These included /r/the_greatawakening, /r/BiblicalQ, /r/Quincels, and 15 other subreddits.

These subreddits were said to be host to numerous violent threats that are rooted in the posts of QAnon. Community moderators repeatedly called for the anonymous posters to stop the threats, but these pleas fell on deaf ears. The threats of violence increased exponentially particularly during the time when the Mueller Investigation was taking place. The people believed that Mueller was not investigating Trump and his associates, rather, he was using this opportunity to look into a global ring of pedophiles that were led by people from the Democratic Party, most notable of which was Hillary Clinton.

The QAnon followers posted threats of killing Clinton particularly when one of Q's posts mentioned that military planes were falling out of the sky because of Clinton's doing. The members of the community were seeking out other members who could kill who they considered were the enemies.

A number of the community members have also been called out for posting misogynistic, racist, and anti-Semitic entries against government officials, members of the media, and prominent Jewish personalities. [47]

The banning shook other communities because the management of Reddit actively hunted down the members of the subreddits that have been shut down to see if they were trying to reform in a different page. Other communities, such as the /r/The_Donald, even started making policies preventing their members from posting anything that mentions Q or QAnon to prevent from getting banned as well.

As a result of this crackdown, QAnon supporters fled to other forum pages to vent their outrage. One user even compared the shutdown to the oppression experienced by

German Jews during the time of Hitler. In the /r/conspiracy community, a user claimed that the banning only gave QAnon more credibility because it and its growing popularity is obviously making some people nervous. Maybe, they claim, the posts of Q were hitting closer to home and they are not happy that more and more people are seeing the truth.

Other community members also voiced out that the QAnon followers were not violent. Some claimed that it was the group promoted by the Democrats that had a track record for real-world violence, not theirs. It was apparent to them that Reddit was cherry-picking only the groups that were anti-Trump and pro-QAnon for its "cleansing" of their website.

This is what QAnon has been telling his followers all along. People who are working for Deep State will try hard to suppress the great awakening. This suppression is why they need to work doubly hard not only to spread the message of Q but also to confuse the operatives of Deep State.

Many consider this move by Reddit as the beginning of the end for QAnon. Where else would his followers get to talk about his breadcrumbs? The truth is, this move only made the QAnon members look for other avenues where they can safely share their messages with like-minded individuals without fear of being hunted and shut down yet again. Some started their own YouTube channels while others started posting on different blogging platforms. So, is it really the end? Or is this just a minor setback for Q and his followers?

It is not just Reddit that has been cracking down on groups that they deem to be spreading extremism and misinformation. Instagram and Facebook, the parent company, have also started banning controversial accounts. They have already banned Laura Loomer, Paul Nehlen, Milo Yiannopoulos, Alex Jones, Paul Joseph Watson, and Infowars. The platforms also banned Louis Farrakhan. He is the leader of the Nation of Islam and has been cited repeatedly for making anti-Semitic statements.

As for Infowars, this website has been handed the strictest banning. The two platforms promised to immediately remove posted contents that are featuring videos, articles, or radio segments from Infowars. The only time that reposting would be allowed is if it is meant to condemn the content. Facebook also promised to get rid of any groups that are meant to conduct events promoting any of the figures that have been banned.

Infowars and Alex Jones have also been banned by Twitter, Apple, and YouTube. As for Yiannopoulos, Loomer, Nehlen, Farrakhan, and Watson were all personally banned on Facebook. This means any accounts that they set up, or set up in their likeness, shall immediately be removed. Their Instagram accounts though remain up.

While bakers continued to try to reach out to the other members of the movement using other platforms, the options are becoming fewer. In January of 2019, YouTube tweaked its recommendation algorithm as part of their crackdown on videos that are deemed to be "conspiracy-laden".

This means YouTube will no longer list these controversial videos on the sidebar. It is not just QAnon related videos that are getting sidelined by YouTube. Any video that is about 9/11 truthers, flat earth, or fake miracle cures will no longer be recommended. The implementation of these changes will be done through machine learning and actual people doing the tagging.

The big issue here is, who gets to decide when a video contains something that is labeled as a conspiracy theory? History has proven to us that there are some notions that were thought to be conspiracies and end up being proven to be truths.

Even Facebook is working hard to prevent groups from spreading memes and images that spread what they deemed to be debunked hoaxes. In September of 2018, Facebook rolled out a tool which they call Rosetta. This tool automatically detects posts containing images that violate their policies regarding hate speech and discredited hoaxes.

The members of the QAnon movement tested the prowess of Rosetta by uploading videos and memes with deliberately wonky texts, obscured fonts, and backward writings. While these techniques are not yet tested sufficiently to conclude if they can really fool Rosetta, QAnon members are confident that they can think of other ways to go around Facebook's tighter measures.

With the crackdown on posting and sharing of QAnon posts on various social media platforms, the members had to find another avenue to be able to reach the other followers of the movement. This was one of the reasons why QDrops was created. QDrops is an application that pushes alerts whenever there are any new developments concerning QAnon.

It is a 99-cent application that was launched by a couple from North Carolina. Richard Brown and his wife, Adalita, created this application without expecting it to grow as popular as it would. It reached the top 10 of all the paid Apple applications and was able to get the top position in the entertainment category for that year.

However, in the middle of 2018, NBC News contacted Apple to inquire as to why they are allowing such an application to be sold on their App Store despite it violating a few guidelines. This led to Apple pulling the app from its store. For the meantime, the app can still be bought from the Google Play Store.

What's questionable is that Apple is not even sure which of their guidelines was violated by QDrops. Eddy Cue, a representative of Apple, simply stated that they believe that hate speech and white supremacist speech is not something that they believe should be allowed to stay out there.

Followers of the QAnon movement see this move as another step in suppressing the truth that Q is sharing with the world. It is difficult to pinpoint who paid Apple to pull the app from their store. But what is for sure is they had to shell out a significant amount considering how much the app is bringing in for the company. This is why QAnon followers have concluded that the pulling of the app must have been an order that came from the top. The amount that had to be paid is nothing considering how rich Deep State's puppet masters are. It would have been a small amount for them.

Besides these social media platforms, Q followers are worrying that even the groups' new home could also soon be censored. After the Christchurch massacre, it was discovered that the killer posted his manifesto on 8chan. Because the horrific incident attracted the attention of people worldwide, the uproar for the website to enforce stricter rules in censoring the contents was considerable.

According to Jasmine Garsd, an NPR personality, it was 8chan that allowed the shooter to post the link to his livestream of the attack on Facebook. She believes that the anger of the victim's family and the community might be enough to get the imageboard website pulled down. As it is, 8chan is already banned from New Zealand's and Australia's servers. Analysts believe that banning this particular site will be a little more difficult in countries like America. This knowledge is good enough for the Q followers for the meantime. Besides, there are still some avenues left for them. They can still use personal blog sites and Instagram accounts to be able to share their theories.

ANONYMOUS PROMISES TO GET Q

"Anonymous" is not a term that is exclusive to QAnon members and followers. It was first associated with an older group. The popular cyberactivist group, Anonymous, has issued a threat to the members of QAnon. They pledged that they will do everything that they can in order to sabotage the group's operation and expose its members. In a 3-minute long video, a person wearing a Guy Fawkes mask explained that they plan to wreck QAnon.

In June of 2018, The Twitter profile @YourAnonNews gave a signal boost to the hashtags #OpQAnon and #OpQ. This was a go-ahead gesture for the members of the hacking collective to start with their plans. This account was said to be the most reliable source of information regarding Anonymous. According to one spokesperson, the group is unhappy with QAnon because it takes advantage of the poorly educated and the misinformed.

This is not the first time that this group, composed of skilled hackers, decided to take down an influential entity. As a form of protest, the group launches leaks and "denial of service" online attacks targeting the Ku Klux Klan, ISIS, and the Church of Scientology. The group even managed to shut down the websites of both the United Nations' and the CIA's. They were also instrumental in getting

WikiLeaks to publish emails that they stole from a global intelligence firm, Stratfor.

What made Anonymous even more incensed was the perceived co-opting of their brand. They think that the original QAnon author tried to associate himself with the collective. They claimed that they do not like any form of political agenda and the fact that the author used the name Anon is a serious affront to them.

So far, the group was able to take over several hashtags that were often used by QAnon followers. They also managed to dox over a hundred QAnon members. This could just be the beginning of their offensive. So far, it seems all cyberwar for now. However, Anonymous is not just a small threat. When they declared war against the Ku Klux Klan, not only were they able to knock the group's website offline, they also compromised the group members' emails and conducted harassments of the said members over the phone.

If the members of Anonymous took this war seriously, they can do some major damage on QAnon and his progress in exposing the truths to the public. While many believe that Anonymous will not accept Deep State's payment, it is not a long shot that Deep State had a hand in this.

It is surprising how all this bad press has affected the number of people who believe in Q and his messages. Are these separate and unrelated incidents or is this Deep State's planned attack to stop Q from gaining more followers? If so, one could only imagine what more Deep State can do in order to permanently silence QAnon.

CONCLUSION

For the longest time, any idea that goes against what is considered the norm is labeled as crazy. If it seems implausible, then it must be a conspiracy theory. But history has proven that some of the theories that were considered foolish before have been proven to be valid eventually.

There was the uncovering of the MK-Ultra project, the actual surveillance of personalities like John Lennon, the Mockingbird Project, and the discovery that people are looking through your web camera to spy on you. Thus, while the concept of an insider of the White House systematically leaking information in order to rally the supporters of President Trump is not that out of this world.

The ideas that are presented by Q and that are disseminated by his bakers all seem outlandish. They are so "out there" that people think, only a crazy person would believe this. But, there must be a reason why it was able to push out of the confines of a relatively unknown message board into mainstream social media.

Maybe, despite all the outrageousness, people were able to see some truth. People are more perceptive of these because they had their eyes opened for them. Not all, but a considerable number has joined the movement.

The QAnon movement which pushed forward several controversial ideas and what seemed like military intelligence through an imageboard website has thrived and persisted despite seeing many of its leader's claims running contrary to what happened in reality.

Q told his followers that Clinton was the head of a pedophilia ring. He maintains that Obama has been making deals with other country and helping them develop nuclear arms so that the world can be plunged with the permanent fear of being at the brink of war. He claimed that J.P. Morgan somehow had something to do with the sinking of the Titanic just to get rid of his rivals. His notions are alleged truths that have been swirling out there for the longest time.

When Q claimed that Hillary Clinton is set to be arrested for working together with the Russian government, among many other wrongdoings, nothing actually happened. Clinton is still free. The Democrats are still in power. The Rothschilds and George Soros still have their money and power. In fact, the only ruling family that may have taken a little bit of a dive in this entire thing is the House of Saud.

Misplaced expectations and failed predictions may have disappointed some followers, but their numbers certainly aren't significantly reduced. What may have done the damage though are the attacks of mainstream media. With their effort to uncover who Q is, by disseminating the theories that Q is just a game gone awry or a publicity stunt taken too far, and by highlighting the violent acts that are associated to the QAnon movement, Q has definitely lost a number of believers. The constant bad press has also prompted various platforms, the ones that QAnon had to work so hard to infiltrate, to crackdown on Q's online presence. Reddit has banned its subreddit boards, YouTube removes videos about Q's drops, users can't even share theories about QAnon breadcrumbs on your Facebook and Twitter accounts.

Many are now wondering whether this phenomenon is about to bite the dust. Is QAnon losing traction or is it like a phoenix situation where he has to let everything burn before he can rise out of the ashes? Q has already revealed to us instances when he seemed so wrong only to reveal that he knew something right all along. What is Q's next move? All we can do is wait and see.

Sources:

1 - https://www.newyorker.com/science/elements/looking-for-life-on-a-flat-earth

2 - https://en.wikipedia.org/wiki/Project_MKUltra

3 - https://www.npr.org/templates/story/story.php?storyId=130401193?storyId=130401193

4 - https://www.rd.com/advice/work-career/laptop-camera/

5 - https://newlaborforum.cuny.edu/2018/08/28/is-there-a-deep-state/

6 - https://www.countable.us/articles/6610-qanon-countable-q-anon

7 - https://www.theepochtimes.com/the-q-phenomenon_2581642.html

8 - https://www.dailydot.com/layer8/who-is-q-anon/

9 - https://en.wikipedia.org/wiki/4chan

10 - https://steemit.com/nomorefakenews/@gomeravibz/qanon-is-real-confirmed-by-trump-himself-in-a-coded-tweet

11 - https://en.wikipedia.org/wiki/Hillary_Clinton_email_controversy

12 - https://www.nbcnews.com/storyline/smart-facts/what-wikileaks-everything-you-need-know-n869556

13 - https://www.politifact.com/truth-o-meter/article/2016/dec/05/how-pizzagate-went-fake-news-real-problem-dc-busin/

14 - https://www.washingtonpost.com/news/local/wp/2016/12/04/d-c-police-respond-to-report-of-a-man-with-a-gun-at-comet-ping-pong-restaurant/?utm_term=.f044161ca0a6

15 - https://gizmodo.com/pizzagaters-arent-giving-this-shit-up-1789692422

16 - https://www.nbcnews.com/tech/social-media/pizzagate-conspiracy-video-posted-youtube-account-alleged-arsonist-s-parents-n971891

17 - https://www.buzzfeednews.com/article/salvadorhernandez/pizzagate-conspiracy-comet-ping-pong-fire-dc-arrest

18 - https://www.nbcnews.com/tech/tech-news/what-qanon-guide-conspiracy-theory-taking-hold-among-trump-supporters-n897271

19 - Davis, Deborah (1979). Katharine The Great: Katharine Graham and The Washington Post. Harcourt Brace Jovanovich. ISBN 0151467846.

20 - https://www.washingtonpost.com/local/long-ago-wiretap-inspires-a-battle-with-the-cia-for-more-information/2013/03/02/8ebaa924-77b0-11e2-aa12-e6cf1d31106b_story.html?noredirect=on

21 – Williams, Paul L. (2015). Operation Gladio: The Unholy Alliance between the Vatican, the CIA, and the Mafia. Prometheus Books. ISBN 1616149744.

22 - https://www.breitbart.com/politics/2017/08/04/sessions-orders-doj-recount-slush-fund-payments-leftists/

23 - https://nypost.com/2016/10/09/the-sex-slave-scandal-that-exposed-pedophile-billionaire-jeffrey-epstein/

24 -

https://www.vox.com/2018/12/3/18116351/jeffrey-epstein-trump-clinton-labor-secretary-acosta

25 - https://www.dailydot.com/layer8/whidbey-island-missile-air-force-one/

26 - https://www.nytimes.com/2017/05/17/us/seth-rich-dnc-wikileaks.html

27 - https://theintercept.com/2018/02/02/nunes-memo-fisa-trump-russia/

28 - https://www.history.com/news/titanic-sinking-conspiracy-myths-jp-morgan-olympic

29 - https://www.exopolitics.org/qanon-rothschilds-satanism-trumps-alliance-putin/

30 - https://www.exopolitics.org/tag/red-october/

31 - https://www.smithsonianmag.com/history/leaks-and-the-law-the-story-of-thomas-drake-14796786/

32 - http://thedailyhaze.com/bad-self-eater-anti-abortion-video/

33 - https://www.dailydot.com/layer8/alex-jones-qanon-compromised/

34 - https://www.macrumors.com/2008/10/03/fake-rumors-of-steve-jobs-heart-attack-circulate/

35 - https://www.nbcnews.com/tech/tech-news/how-three-conspiracy-theorists-took-q-sparked-qanon-n900531

36 - https://i.redd.it/6zq652jwnhuz.png

37 - https://steemit.com/hundredthmonkey/@dreamtime/high-level-insider-ama-from-4chan-transcripts-easy-to-read-not-in-4chan-form-part-6-7-11-16-4

38 - https://www.nbcnews.com/tech/tech-news/how-three-conspiracy-theorists-took-q-sparked-qanon-n900531

39 - https://www.nbcnews.com/tech/tech-news/youtube-search-results-list-celebrities-hijacked-conspiracy-theorists-n895926

40 - https://www.nbcnews.com/tech/social-

media/arizona-veterans-group-finds-homeless-camp-fuels-new-pizzagate-style-n880956

41 - https://www.independent.co.uk/news/world/americas/trump-florida-rally-supporters-cnn-jim-acosta-tampa-maga-a8472436.html

42 - https://www.tampabay.com/news/military/double-trouble-for-broward-deputy-one-patch-for-qanon-conspiracy-another-for-his-swat-team-20181204/

43 - https://www.dailydot.com/layer8/qanon-failed-predictions/

44 - https://www.independent.co.uk/news/world/americas/trump-florida-rally-supporters-cnn-jim-acosta-tampa-maga-a8472436.html

45 - https://www.buzzfeednews.com/article/skbaer/qanon-believer-arrested-hoover-dam

46 - https://www.bbc.com/news/world-us-canada-48231708

47 - https://www.foxnews.com/tech/reddit-bans-qanon-conspiracy-theory-forums